FACTORY OUTLET GUIDE TO THE MIDWEST

FACTORY OUTLET GUIDE TO THE MIDWEST

Illinois, Indiana, Iowa, Michigan
Minnesota, Missouri, Ohio, Wisconsin

by A. Tightwad & A. Pennypincher

A Voyager Book

The Globe Pequot Press

Chester, Connecticut

Library of Congress Cataloging-in-Publication Data

Tightwad, A.
Factory outlet guide to the Midwest: Illinois, Indiana, Iowa, Michigan, Minnesota, Missouri, Ohio, Wisconsin / by A. Tightwad and A. Pennypincher.
p. cm.
"A Voyager book."
ISBN 0-87106-237-2
1. Outlet stores—Middle West—Directories. I. Pennypincher, A. II. Title.
HF5429.4.A14T54 1991
381'.15'02577—dc20 91-4194
CIP

Manufactured in the United States of America
First Edition/First Printing

CONTENTS

INTRODUCTION

Why do factory outlets exist? Outlets are the manufacturers' solution to selling goods that tie up precious money. Some manufacturers find it too costly to send a quality item back through the production line because it's missing a button or to let last year's overproduced style gather dust in the warehouse. And then there are the headaches that manufacturers encounter from ever-larger department store chains that cancel orders, return unsold goods, or carry private label goods. So manufacturers send all this merchandise to an outlet store, where it is labeled as first-quality overruns, seconds, irregulars, or damaged.

Factories in major Midwest cities and other manufacturing centers started the outlet concept years ago. Opening spartan stores usually adjoining their plants, they offered defective but usable goods and excess merchandise. Their employees and sometimes the neighborhood general public had access to the items and snapped up these bargains. The news spread by word of mouth to frugal farmers and cost-conscious city dwellers, who were also eager to save their hard-earned dollars. Manufacturers spruced up sales areas and started to advertise—and factory outlets became part of the shopping scene.

The next step in this evolution was the appearance of factory outlet centers, a group of outlet stores located close to each other. Originally an East Coast phenomenon, the first outlet center opened nearly fifteen years ago in Reading, Pennsylvania, now cited as the birthplace of factory outlet shopping. Consumers looking for bargains flocked to these centers by the busloads.

The success of these centers resulted in the development of well-planned factory outlet malls. Their attraction lies in having plenty of parking, easy accessibility, and a variety of stores. Offering savings from 20 to 75 percent, factory outlet malls are fast becoming bargain-hunting meccas, as their assortment of goods ranges from shelves to shoes and then some. This one-stop-shopping convenience trend has become so popular that across the country there are more than 300 outlet chains with more than 6,000 store locations.

In the land-rich Midwest, factory outlet malls have been cropping up in less-populated areas along the interstates and in tourist spots, so placed to avoid competing with department stores that offer merchandise at retail prices. In fact, the Midwest is such a hotbed for expansion of factory outlet malls that thirty additional outlet malls are planned for the near future.

Individual factory outlets, in contrast, tend to remain in larger cities, the older established centers of commerce. Many are still adjacent to the factory or located as freestanding units. While not as sleek or as attractively decorated as their mall counterparts, they should in no way be overlooked. Low overhead and low-tech merchandising translates into large discounts.

Don't assume, either, that outlet merchandise is low quality or undesirable. Granted, whether shopping at an outlet mall or single-standing outlet, you will find some defective merchandise. But many quality items come from prestigious companies that manufacture well-recognized brand names, and discerning shoppers can separate the wheat from the chaff and come away with great bargains. The bottom line is that outlet merchandise can cost half the retail price.

Just like retail stores, some outlets run annual, clearance, or seasonal sales. An item that may be a good buy at the discounted price then becomes a great buy. Check with your favorite outlets to see if you can tap into this extra bargain bounty. (Regular annual sales at specific outlets are noted in the geographic portion of the book, under the "additional savings" heading. Other outlets may have sales during the year, but if they are not annual events, they are not listed.)

Who shops at factory outlets? You'd be surprised! Some people simply love to bargain shop. Others just can't stand paying full retail price. A third group—some senior citizens, single mothers, or lower-income people—can't afford to purchase full-price goods. At some point, it seems that nearly everyone needs to arm themselves in the battle of the budget. By shopping outlets, the cost of this book can be saved almost instantly. Realistically, it is possible to save 50 percent of your shopping budget.

Even though this book focuses primarily on outlet shopping, a small number of select stores that offer deep discounts are also provided as a reader service. Deep discounters are middlemen that buy merchandise from manufacturers or distributors and then mark it up for resale. Also known as "off-price" stores, they sell for less because their merchandise consists of mostly large-lot buys from manufacturers who need to sell quickly. Some stores that call themselves outlets are in reality "off-price" retailers. Although not true outlets, discounters need not be overlooked if you like their merchandise and prices. After all, our goal is saving money.

One final point: Outlets don't order merchandise in specific styles and sizes; they get what manufacturers can't sell through retail stores. The stock differs from day to day. Keep in mind: If you see it and like it, buy it. The sweater or bedspread that catches your eye today probably won't be there tomorrow.

Planning Your Shopping Trip

Outlet shopping is more productive and less stressful when these few simple guidelines are followed:

Organize yourself before a shopping expedition by setting up a loose-leaf notebook. Establish an index listing birthdays, anniversaries, and other significant dates for friends and family members. Divide the notebook into sections. Set aside a section for each person for whom you shop. In each section, note the person's sizes for various goods, merchandise needed, color preference, favorite brand names and desires. A home section, with room-by-room measurements, prepares you to take advantage of houseware bargains. Keep extra pages in the binder for categories as the need arises. With the information at your fingertips, your shopping expeditions can proceed smoothly.

Jot down prices when shopping at local retail stores. This establishes a retail price comparison so that you can judge the true outlet "deals." It also gives you an idea of current styles and colors.

Keep the *Factory Outlet Guide to the Midwest* in the car while driving to vacation destinations. Check the book or signs posted on the highway to see if you'll be passing near any outlet malls or stores. Refer to the Profiles section of this book to see if a detour is worth your while. A well-planned itinerary or an unexpected detour can lead you to tremendous savings and help defray the cost of your trip.

To keep your budget-conscious life-style going strong even while on vacation, a list of state tourism contacts is included, along with toll-free phone numbers to maximize every savings opportunity. State tourism information centers are a valuable source of cost-saving information. You'll be made aware of less costly overnight accommodations, special discount packages, and reasonably priced restaurants. This translates into more money for shopping. When contacting these agencies, ask for updated outlet information in the area you plan to visit.

Using This Book

To simplify the use of this book, we have divided it into two sections:

1. The Profiles section includes generic information about each outlet in the book. Because outlet names may vary somewhat from one location to another, we have listed name variations in this section to minimize any confusion.

2. Cities are listed in alphabetical order under their appropriate states in the geographic section. Individual outlets and malls are then listed alphabetically under cities. A basic map introducing each state's listings illustrates, in a general way, the location of cities covered in the text.

In compiling data for the book, every attempt to provide accurate information was made. Nevertheless, stores go out of business, they close for vacation, they change business hours, and they move. There is no way to control or predict the ebb and flow of commercial endeavors. Do not go any great distance without first checking whether things have changed since this book was written. Likewise, don't assume that a store is located in an outlet center because a similar center has that store as an anchor establishment. Leasing arrangements vary from state to state and from center to center.

If stores are in an area affected by tourism—as are many near amusement parks and other attractions—their hours fluctuate with the tourism season. Be prepared for reduced hours in the off-season. Many stores accept credit cards; when they do not, the listing will so indicate. Take along cash or your checkbook with at least two forms of proper identification, usually a driver's license and a major credit card. Be aware that some stores do not accept personal checks; look for that information in the listing. Most outlets are fully or partially accessible to handicapped shoppers. An accessibility heading for each outlet or mall indicates the *general* conditions readers will encounter.

Factory outlet shopping is a challenge. In meeting that challenge, you and your budget become the winners. This guide provides you with the winning edge in this ongoing money-saving adventure. Go out, have fun, and save!

State Tourism Information

Illinois Office of Tourism
State of Illinois Center
100 W. Randolf, Suite 3–400
Chicago, IL 60601
(800) 223–0121

Indiana Tourism Division
One North Capitol, Suite 700
Indianapolis, IN 46204
(800) 289–6646

Iowa Division of Tourism
200 E. Grand Avenue
Des Moines, IA 50309
(800) 345–IOWA

Michigan Travel Bureau
P.O. Box 30226
Lansing, MI 48909
(800) 543–2937

Minnesota Office of Tourism
375 Jackson Walkway
250 Skyway Level
St. Paul, MN 55101
(800) 657–3700

Missouri Division of Tourism
P.O. Box 1055
Jefferson City, MO 65102
(800) 877–1234

Ohio Division of Travel
and Tourism
P.O. Box 1001
Columbus, OH 43216–0101
(800) BUCKEYE

Wisconsin Division of Tourism
123 W. Washington Avenue
P.O. Box 7970
Madison, WI 53707
(800) 432–TRIP

Finding New Manufacturers

Many manufacturers are subsidiaries or divisions of large corporations. We include a list of corporate affiliations to enable you to shop with greater knowledge and understanding of the brand names you're likely to find in factory stores.

Knowing corporate affiliations will enable you to anticipate the brand names you can expect to find in a direct factory outlet. For example, suppose you're planning a trip to one of the Oxford Industries, Inc. outlets. In checking the list, you learn that besides Oxford goods you should also find Neon, Lanier Clothes, Oscar de la Renta Clothing, B. J. Design Concepts, Polo for Boys, Holbrook Shirts, Cos Cob Sportswear, JBJ Sportswear, and Merona Sport. Thus, you are able to prepare a comprehensive shopping list before taking a buying trip.

A knowledge of connections among apparel manufacturers will also help you recognize the quality and value of unfamiliar labels. For instance, you may buy Evan Picone apparel because you feel it is well made, but have you ever tried Palm Beach clothing, which is part of the same corporation? When shopping and finding these new labels, you can now take a fresh look at them.

Similarly, if you have outgrown the size range of a favorite manufacturer's apparel, knowing the names of other manufacturers in the same corporation can help you find new clothing with the same quality and value.

This partial list includes some subsidiaries and divisions of corporations that we thought would be of interest to you.

Banister Corporation
- Capezio
- Freeman
- Joyce
- Mushrooms
- Pappagallo
- Red Cross
- Selby

Eire
- Aynsley
- Johnston Brothers
- Waterford
- Wedgwood

Manhattan Corporation
- Anne Klein
- Henry Grethel
- John Henry
- Manhattan
- Perry Ellis

Palm Beach Corporation
- Evan Picone
- Gant
- Haspel
- Palm Beach

Shapely Corporation
- Breckenridge
- Kaspar
- Leslie Fay
- Nolan Miller

VF Corporation
- Bassett Walker
- Heron Cove
- Jantzen
- Kay Windsor
- Lee
- Li'l Lollipop
- Vanity Fair

Warnaco
- Chaps
- Hathaway
- Lauren
- Olga
- Puritan
- Speedo
- White Stag

No outlet owner may purchase inclusion in this book. Inclusion is purely a personal decision on the part of the authors. In addition, some outlets chose not to participate in the compilation of this book, and providing pertinent information was on a purely voluntary basis. Consequently, the extent of information may vary from profile to profile and outlet to outlet.

Authors' visits to stores are unannounced and anonymous so as to avoid special treatment and promotional influence. Future editions of this guide will allow for additions of new factory stores. To have a store considered for inclusion, please address questions or comments to The Globe Pequot Press, Box Q, Chester, Connecticut 06412. All inquiries will be given careful consideration for future editions. References from readers will be greatly appreciated.

PROFILES

Action Housewares
Discounted housewares and cookware.

Adams Factory Shoes
The finest quality men's and women's footwear. Slight blemish defects and overruns of current styles are purchased from the best manufacturers and sold at savings up to 60 percent. In business over 45 years, extra-wide, extra-large, and unusual sizes are a specialty.

Adolfo II
Designer wear for the well-dressed woman, direct from the manufacturer at 20 to 50 percent off. Noted labels include Adolfo II, Rafael, Donna Tora, and Dressy Tessy.

Aileen Stores
Manufacturer-owned and -operated women's sportswear in petite, missy, and women's sizes. American-made, first-quality goods are discounted from 35 to 70 percent.

Ambassador Crystal
Crystal and gold items offered at a discount.

Ambrosia Chocolate & Cocoa
Fine chocolates, cocoa, and confections; fresh homemade fudge and candies plus baking- and candy-making supplies; handmade gifts.

American Bicycle Manufacturing
First-quality aluminum mountain bikes, tandems, seat posts, and stems are offered direct from the manufacturer.

American Commodore Tuxedo
New and used men's formal wear discounted 40 percent.

American Tourister
Top-quality luggage and travel products are discounted from 40 to 70 percent. Items include "gorilla tough" hard-sided luggage, soft-sided luggage, attaché cases, and sports bags in a variety of sizes. Ships anywhere in the United States.

Ameri-Tux
Bill Blass, Christian Dior, Pierre Cardin, and After Six formal wear at discounted everyday rentals of 40 percent and more.

Amy Stoudt
Personal service and first-quality fashions for the large-size woman in sizes 14W–32W. Current season clothing for work, evening, or weekends is discounted from 20 to 50 percent off everyday prices.

Andercraft Woods
Direct from the factory, first-quality, nationally sold Wisconsin white cedar planters, mailboxes, birdhouses, feeders, and nativity stables at savings up to 50 percent.

Anderson Fabrics
Makers of top-quality interior designer household fabrics as well as blinds, shades, and verticals, all at 50 percent off suggested retail. Coordinated wallpaper, dust ruffles, pillow shams, quilted spreads, and curtains are carried. Special order fabrics and custom labor services are 25 percent off retail. Drapery hardware is 15 percent off.

Anko Also
High-fashion Anko women's apparel with an extensive accessory collection to coordinate, direct from the manufacturer from 20 to 50 percent off.

Anne Klein
Manufacturer's savings up to 50 percent on first-quality Anne Klein II apparel and accessories including jewelry, perfume, watches, and handbags.

Annie's Son Shoes
Name-brand shoes for men, women, and children plus accessories.

Arbetman Brothers & Blaire

Factory owned and operated, first-quality ladies' outerwear is available year-round with discounts from 50 to 75 percent.

Argenti

A fabulous selection of ladies' apparel priced from 33 to 75 percent off for the well-dressed woman. This high-quality manufacturer, noted for silk garments in misses', petite, and plus sizes, carries well-made dresses, blouses, suits, evening wear, and accessories.

Artfare

Original art from the artist directly to you. Gifts, collectibles, crafts, and photographs, as well as arts and craft supplies. Classes are also available.

Athletic Shoe Factory

Clothing, accessories, and brand-name athletic shoes for the serious and part-time athlete.

Aunt Mary's Yarns

Needlework supplies such as yarns, crewel, and needlepoint, along with craft materials, art supplies, and silk and dried floral supplies at discounted prices.

Bag & Baggage

Luggage and handbag outlet featuring a complete selection of famous-name luggage, business cases, handbags, and small leather goods from 20 to 50 percent off suggested retail.

B & J Sales

The world's finest fragrances discounted up to 75 percent. Designer names without the designer price like Estée Lauder, Gucci, Bijan, and other French and U.S. favorites. An inventory of more than 15,000 fragrances plus cosmetics and accessories at discount prices.

Banister Shoes

Factory direct prices, with savings up to 50 percent on Capezio, Pappagallo, Mushrooms, Liz Claiborne, Freeman, and nearly forty other manufacturers of men's and women's name-brand casual and athletic footwear.

Barbizon
Fine lingerie direct from the manufacturer at savings of 30 to 60 percent. Quality fabrication offers detailing, embroidery, and laces.

Bargain Fabrics
The place to find quality fabrics and notions at bargain prices. Their large assortment includes foam, patterns, lace trims, ribbons, knit T-shirts, ribbing, and a variety of fabrics, and upholstery/drapery material.

Bass Shoes/G. H. Bass
Savings of 25 percent or more off the retail price on full-grain leather Weejuns, Bucs, Sunjuns sandals, and other classic footwear and accessories. Merchandise has the quality and style that has been a Bass tradition for more than a hundred years.

Beauty Fair USA
More than 2,500 professional beauty supplies at discount prices. Products by leading manufacturers such as Clairol, Revlon, L'Oréal, Zotos, and Hayashi. Shampoos, styling aids, appliances, and skin- and nail-care products not found in drug or discount stores.

Becca
Unique, contemporary women's apparel.

Bemidji Woolen Mills
First- and second-quality men's and women's woolen garments, including wool sports shirts and heavy-lined hunting coats are available at 20 to 50 percent below retail. Some are made in the mill; others are name brands such as Woolrich, Pendleton, and Hudson Bay. Yarns by the pound, sweaters, wool batting, and remnants are also stocked.

Benetton
Save up to 50 percent on a large selection of summer and winter international clothing fashions, available year-round.

Bergquist Imports, Inc.
The factory-owned outlet features first quality and seconds in Scandinavian design dinnerware, mugs, tiles, and plates. Discounts average 30 percent.

BG Chicago

Women's classic and contemporary coordinating seasonal sportswear and dresses with some samples. Labels include Robbie Sport, Robbie Bee, Terry & Peone. Jewelry, fragrances, handbags, and belts are also stocked.

Big and Better

Plus-size discounts on plus-size, better quality fashions for the full-figured woman. Name brands include Bonnie and Bill, Sasson, Rafaella, Intuitions, and more.

Bike Nashbar

Everything for the cyclist, discounted from the catalog. Apparel, equipment, bicycles, accessories, and footwear for men and women.

Black & Decker

Small appliances, tools, and hardware at up to 35 percent off every day.

Blume Jewelers

Discounted from 20 to 30 percent, first-quality Citizen and Seiko watches, Colibri goods, Landstrum Black Hills gold, Speidel watchbands, and Artcarved wedding bands are available. Watch and jewelry repairs are offered.

Bon Worth

Name-brand missy and women's sportswear. Discounts can run up to 90 percent. Bon Worth products are from 30 to 60 percent off regular retail.

Bookland

More than 100,000 books from selected *New York Times* best-sellers to magazines and paperbacks. Everything in the store is discounted up to 80 and 90 percent.

Book Warehouse

National deep-discount chain that sells new books at 50 to 90 percent off publisher's suggested retail prices. Reading material for all tastes including children's books, cookbooks, and self-improvement selections.

Bootery
Up to 50 percent savings every day on men's and women's brand-name fashion footwear. Handbags and accessories are also value priced.

Boyd's Crystal Art Glass
Factory-direct, first-quality collectible antique glass reproductions in a wide spectrum of colors. Take a free tour and watch craftsmen at one of America's most respected glass factories.

Brands
Discounted quality apparel and accessories for men and women, all at savings of 30 to 70 percent off retail. Brand names featured are Perry Ellis, Chaps by Ralph Lauren, Nancy Heller, Sanyo, Bill Blass, Michii Moon, Leon Levin, and Lakeland.

Brass Factory Outlet
High-quality solid-brass accessories for home and office available at factory-direct prices. Nautical accessories, gifts, and decorations to choose from, too.

The Brighter Side
Exclusive collection of oil lamps and oils at manufacturer's discounts of up to 70 percent every day. Accessory parts such as wicks, burners, and chimneys are stocked along with sconces and floral accent rings.

Bristol County
Ladies' tailored American-made suits, skirts, slacks, and blazers direct from the manufacturer.

Brooks Athletic Outlet
Athletic footwear and apparel.

Brooks Boot & Shoe
A true outlet in back of the factory. Save from 20 to 50 percent on footwear for the whole family.

Brownberry Bakery
Substantial savings of 30 to 40 percent off retail on bakery overruns.

All-natural breads, rolls, croutons, stuffing, and other fine bakery products are brought in fresh daily.

Bruce Alan Bags, Etc.
Indulge in luxury leather handbags from the finest designers at savings of 25 to 45 percent off regular retail price. Choose from handbags, accessories, wallets, attaché cases, travel accessories, and hard-to-find notions.

Bugle Boy
Bugle Boy and Vincente Nesi contemporary sportswear, shoes, and accessories. Factory owned and operated, with savings of 20 to 60 percent.

Burlington Coat
Famous-maker women's, children's, and men's wear, mostly first quality and current season. Coats, dresses, sportswear, handbags, and a full line of brand-name shoes, linens, and bath accessories are discounted from 25 to 70 percent. Also London Fog raincoats for men and women at tremendous savings.

Burlington Shoe Store
Savings of 20 to 60 percent over other retail stores on famous-brand shoes for men, women, and children. Choose from dress or casual styles and a large selection of brand-name athletic shoes for men and women.

Burnham Glove
Direct from the manufacturer, more than 1,000 styles of gloves and mittens. First quality, irregular, and buy-outs of dress, golf, garden, ski, work, and play gloves for men, women, and children. Discounts range from 50 to 75 percent.

Calvin Klein
Men's and women's designer sportswear at mostly 50 percent off. Calvin Klein jeans at savings of 30 to 70 percent.

Cambridge Dry Goods
Updated traditional women's sportswear, activewear, and career wear

at savings of 30 to 70 percent on Cambridge Dry Goods, Cambridge Sports Club, Cambridge Spirit, and J. J. Farner labels.

Campus
Men's and boys' first-quality apparel with manufacturer discounts from 40 to 70 percent off nationally advertised retail prices. Look for men's regular, big, and tall sizes and boys' sizes 4 to 20 in Campus, Letigre, and J. J. Cochran.

Cape Craftsmen
Gifts and home accessories at 20 to 50 percent off regular retail. Choose from a wide selection of wooden ware, country lace, potpourri, candles, crystal, wicker, dolls, and linens.

Cape Isle Knitters
Top quality, name-brand sweaters and knit goods in 100 percent cotton. Men and women save with direct manufacturer discounts from 30 to 50 percent.

Capezio Shoes
Take the pinch out of buying this famous manufacturer's women's shoes. Most stores carry Bandolino, Capezio, Gundie, Evan Picone, Anne Klein, Garolini, and Calvin Klein shoes.

Captree/Vanderbilt
Women's, missy, and junior sportswear and accessories with savings of 25 to 60 percent.

Carlson's Christmas Collection
Where Christmas lives all year round. Exquisite handmade accessories and giftware plus merchandise from Fitz and Floyd, Baldwin, and Virginia Metalcrafters.

Carole Hochman Lingerie
Direct from the manufacturer, everyday savings of 40 to 70 percent on America's leading fashion intimate apparel. Name brands include Christian Dior, Carole Hochman, Sara Beth lingerie, and Lily of France bras.

Carolina Designs

Lenox candles of every size and description, plus candle holders, flower rings, Carolina soaps, bathroom accessories, and gift items always 30 to 70 percent off. Lenox is the largest candle manufacturer in the country.

Carousel Animal Fair

It's a real zoo here, with plush, cuddly stuffed animals. The manufacturer sells overstock and discontinued styles at 60 percent off, often more. T-shirts, nightshirts, and slippers, even overstuffed animal paw-type slippers, plus cartoon characters, round out the selection of merchandise.

Carter's Childrenswear

A full line of children's playwear, sleepwear, and underwear, newborn to size 14; also complete layette products. Save 20 to 60 percent direct from the manufacturer.

Casual Male

Contemporary, casual-look fashions for men of all ages. Save 30 to 60 percent off department store prices.

Casual Male Big and Tall

Affordable brand-name fashions for big and tall men of all ages.

Chicago Records

Low, low prices and a great selection. More than 8,000 cassette tapes, 6,000 compact discs, T-shirts, and posters plus audio and video accessories.

The Children's Outlet

Quality clothing for boys and girls from newborn through size 14. Famous brands like OshKosh, Health-Tex, and Baby Togs are discounted from 20 to 40 percent.

China Plus

Fine Sango dinnerware from the manufacturer at 20 to 70 percent off. Flatware, drinkware, server pieces, and gifts from Nikko, International

China, Dansk, Nancy Calhoun, F. B. Rogers, and Crisa are also sold at a discount.

C. J. Chips
Regular, big, and tall sizes of suits, sport coats, slacks, outerwear, and furnishings for men. In-store tailor.

Claires Clearance
Ladies' and girls' jewelry and fashion accessories at affordable prices.

Clothes Connection
Junior and missy fashion in sizes 1 through 18 with savings of 15 to 60 percent. Merchandise includes sportswear, swimwear, jeans, accessories, and more.

Clothes Outs
In-season, current, first-quality, brand-name sportswear for men and women discounted from 20 to 50 percent or more every day.

The Clothes Store
The ladies' better fashion discounter carrying name brands such as Misty Harbor, Cos Cob, Russ, Leslie Fay, Career, Bleyle, and more. Savings run from 30 to 50 percent.

Clothesworks
An outstanding assortment of ladies' clothing at savings of at least 30 percent.

Cluett
Manufacturer of famous family apparel offers brand names like Arrow, Gold Toe, Saturdays, Sundays Sportswear, Alexander Julian, RPM, Burberry shirts, and women's sportswear at savings of 40 percent. Merchandise is first quality, seasonal overruns. Additional savings on select irregulars.

Coffee Boutique
Gourmet coffees and teas plus accessory items, potpourri, gift items, coffee filters, and coffee grinders.

The Coffee Tree
Savings on Melitta products, coffee grinders, and unique coffee mugs. More than fifty varieties of the finest gourmet coffee and tea.

The Company Store
Large selection of down-filled coats, jackets, vests, and booties. Company Store label items at a minimum of 50 percent off.

The Cookie Jar Cookie Outlet
Rippin' Good bulk cookies at savings up to 65 percent and more than one hundred different cookie jars.

Corning/Revere
Excellent savings on Corning glass products such as Corningware, Pyrex, Corelle plus the broadest assortment of Revere accessories.

Cosco
Cosco folding furniture, tray tables, counter and step stools plus carts are available direct from the manufacturer at 50 to 75 percent off suggested retail. Most merchandise is first quality. Some pieces are returned goods inspected for damage and sold at further discounts.

Cotton Mill Stores
Towels, sheets, curtains, linens, bedspreads, and much more at savings up to 70 percent. Mostly first-quality goods with some slight irregulars direct from the manufacturer.

Country Source
Country crafts and gifts.

Crate and Barrel
A huge selection of gourmet cookware, glassware, stemware, bedding, and other accessories with savings from 10 to 70 percent. The bargains are on seconds, irregulars, imperfects, end-of-season goods, samples, and discounted merchandise.

Crawford's Linens
Goods for kitchen, bedroom, and bath. First-quality merchandise, as

well as irregulars from name-brand and off-brand manufacturers. Discounts are from 20 to 70 percent.

Crazy Horse
Contemporary sweaters and sportswear in women's sizes 4 to 16. Select group of men's sweaters.

Create-a-Book
Original, personalized thirty-six-page children's storybooks. Children's name, age, hometown, friends, and family are worked into the story line. Other personalized products.

Creations by Elaine
Custom floral and interior designs plus gifts and decorative accessories, mostly handmade by floral designer/interior decorator Elaine Wolven. Goods are all first quality and are discounted 25 percent.

Creative Touch
Accessories for the home. Brass, gifts, and silk/satin floral arrangements and wedding flowers at reasonable prices.

Cricketeer For Her
Direct from the factory, a division of Joseph & Feiss, with savings of 50 percent. First-quality selection of suits, slacks, blouses, dresses, and coats plus a full line of hosiery, handbags, and accessories.

Crown Jewels
Quality, selection, and value on fine fashion jewelry. Most items offered at 50 percent off the ticketed price.

Crystal Works
Elegant accent pieces, home decorating accessories, and tableware. Significant savings from 20 to 60 percent on Nachtmann's finest quality full-lead European crystal.

C.S.O.
Junior fashions—sportswear, dresses, jackets, coats, lingerie, accessories, and more—at 20 to 70 percent off retail prices.

Dallas Shoes

First-quality buyouts on name-brand shoes for men and women. Famous labels like Anne Klein, 9 West, Calico, Bandolino, Stacey Adams, Nunn Bush, and Giorgio Brutini are discounted from 50 to 70 percent. Accessories, purses, socks, jewelry, and other items are also discounted

danray Lingerie

Sleepwear from gowns, sleepshirts, and baby dolls to cotton pajamas in sizes S, M, L, and 1X through 3X. Sundresses, robes, slouch jackets, slips, underpants, and hosiery are also stocked.

Dansk

Seconds, overstocks, and limited-edition classic Dansk designs in flatware, glassware, cookware, dinnerware, and gifts are discounted up to 60 percent.

Dayton's Outlet

Dented items, discontinued styles, and returned goods, all culled from Dayton's retail stores, are stocked at their outlet. Look for furniture, electronics, appliances, carpeting, and rugs. Good deals get better during "Warehouse Sales."

Designer's Outlet

Better misses', petite, and half-size U.S.-made dresses, suits, and sportswear. Merchandise is mostly first quality with some samples, irregulars, and occasional closeouts. Among the brand names, you'll find Caron, Henry Lee, Terry, Robbie Bee, and Action Gear. Costume jewelry and boutique items are also sold at low prices.

Diamonds Unlimited

Buy at the same wholesale prices that retail jewelers pay from the manufacturer of fine jewelry items.

Dickens Discount Books

New York Times best-sellers in hardcover and paperback, plus other books, all at tremendous savings.

The Discounter
Closeouts, overstocks, odd lots, and liquidations of tools, sporting goods, automotive supplies, groceries, toys, and electronics. Bargains galore are available for the entire family.

District Factory Outlet
New furniture and mattresses are purchased by the trailerload from factory floors. Bedroom, living room, and dining room sets, lamps, bunk beds, recliners, and more are among the goods available. The first-quality merchandise is discounted from 30 to 40 percent off retail.

Dr. Tavel's One Hour Optical
"One-hour glasses without the one-hour price." Prices are generally 20 to 70 percent lower than comparable retail prices on glasses, contact lenses, and eye exams. Goods all first quality. Special offers like the "$1.00 spare."

Dollar Super Store
Closeout merchandise at closeout prices, up to 87 percent off. There's a little of everything: food, clothing, dishes, cosmetics, tools, and much more.

Dress Barn
Name-brand women's fashion labels, always discounted from 20 to 50 percent. Labels like Liz Claiborne, Silk and Company, Guess, Nilani, and many more provide a wide variety of updated fashions.

Dress Barn Woman
Sizes 14 to 24 of name-brand women's fashion labels, similar to those at Dress Barn.

Drug Emporium
"Savings so big you need a shopping cart." First-quality, name-brand health and beauty aids, school and office supplies, greeting cards, cosmetics, fragrances, and cleaning supplies are discounted from 20 to 50 percent every day.

Dunn Woodcrafters
Locally handcrafted folk art, wooden decorative accessories, framed matted prints, statuary, and small furniture items to beautify the home.

Eagle Clothes
Name-brand, designer, and Eagle factory menswear discounted 20 to 50 percent every day. Alteration services available at cost.

Eagle's Eye
Ladies' designer fashions from the famous manufacturer at 40 to 60 percent off. Sportswear, activewear, and career wear in overproduced colors and styles with some irregulars.

Eddie Bauer
Real Eddie Bauer at unreal savings of 40 to 70 percent. Merchandise is first quality and slightly flawed overstock apparel and gear from national catalog and retail stores.

E. J. Plum
Designer socks deliciously priced.

Ekco Houseware
Baker's Secret and Best Results bakeware seconds are discounted up to 50 percent. Other closeouts and seconds from the Ekco Housewares product line are available at a discount.

El-Bee Shoes
Men's and women's famous-brand first-quality and buyout shoes like Reebok, Nike, L. A. Gear, Hush Puppies, Florsheim, Dingo, Calico, Connie, Joyce, Papagallo, and many others are discounted everyday 15 to 60 percent off department store prices.

Enchanted Jewelry
Real leaves and shells preserved in 24K gold. Custom-made chains of 24K gold bonded. Imported 14K-gold jewelry and fine Austrian crystal.

Etienne Aigner
Women's quality fashion footwear at 30 percent off.

European Collections/Oleg Cassini
Savings on ladies' fashion blouses, sportswear, dresses, leathers, and evening wear.

Evan Picone/Izod

First-quality name-brand tailored clothing, sportswear, and accessories for men and women, all current-season fashions. Labels include Evan Picone, Palm Beach, Gant, Eagle, and Izod. Factory-direct savings at 30 to 70 percent off suggested retail prices.

Everitt Knitting Co.

Straight from the factory, Everitt Knitting Company offers first quality, seconds, and overruns in knit headwear, scarves, gloves, socks, and garments. Discounts average 50 to 75 percent. Knit fabric, trims, yarns, and notions are also available.

Factory Card Outlet

Quality party supplies, gift wrap, and gifts at a discount of 20 percent off the suggested retail price with greeting cards discounted at 50 percent.

Factory Direct

Outlet for Lancaster Colony Corporation, which owns Indiana Glass, Candle-lite, Marzetti Salad Dressing, Mountain Top Pies, and Pretty Products interior car accessories. Some first-quality merchandise is available. The majority is buy-outs, closeouts, and discontinued items, particularly of Candle-lite and Indiana Glass products. Savings go as high as 70 percent off retail.

Factory Glass, Candle & Gift Outlet

L. E. Smith glass, pottery, and assorted glass products are discounted 32 percent on first-quality items, 55 percent on seconds and closeouts. Candles and gifts are discounted 22 to 50 percent daily.

Factory Linens

True outlet that carries kitchen, table, bed, and bath linens from Ritz and Ritz Royal with 30 to 40 percent discounts.

Factory Shoe Outlet

Discounted shoes for women and children. Brand names include Jumping Jacks, Little Capezios, Nike, Reebok, Bernardo, and Moxees.

Famous Designer Outlet

Men's and women's casual and career apparel discounted every day.

Famous Footwear

Guarantees the best prices on brand-name shoes for the entire family. Dress, casual, boots, and athletic shoes are stocked. Featured brands include Reebok, Nike, Adidas, Jacqueline, Mushrooms, Candies, Nunn Bush, and more at everyday savings of 10 to 50 percent.

Famous Name Gifts

Something for every age group from stickers and buttons to fireplace tools and German imports. Popular gift items are priced at savings of 25 to 50 percent. Solid brass items, porcelain dolls, and Christmas ornaments are offered at 50 percent of marked retail price.

F & M Distributors

Noticeably cheaper than discount stores on first-quality health and beauty aids, cosmetics, pet supplies, film processing, greeting cards, and so much more. Savings average around 35 to 70 percent. Double coupons and 10 percent savings for senior citizens are offered.

Fanny Farmer Shops

Almost perfect Fanny Farmer chocolates, fudge, nuts, bulk chocolates, holiday, and nonchocolate candy at 25 to 50 percent off suggested retail prices.

Farah

Farah men's and boys' apparel. Boys' sizes 4 to 12, prep, husky, and young men's sizes. Farah brands include Farah, W. F., Savanne, E'Joven, and N.P.W. direct from the manufacturer with discounts from 35 to 40 percent.

Farberware

Manufacturer's direct prices on Farberware cookware, well below suggested retail.

Faribo Woolens/Woolen Mill

A wide selection of first-quality, irregular, and discounted mill blankets and throws. Famous-maker men's, women's, and children's clothing runs 15 to 25 percent below department store prices.

Farmer's Pride Cheese, Inc.
Top-grade Wisconsin Colby, Monterey Jack, and flavored longhorn cheeses are available at this manufacturer's outlet, including their trademark Co-Jack longhorn. Discounts are based on size and quantity, but prices are considerably less than retail.

Fashion Factory Outlet
Women's current-style designer-label apparel at 20 to 70 percent off suggested retail. Office, dress, or casual wear is stocked.

Fashion Flair
Izod LaCoste, Ship 'n Shore, and Monet apparel and accessories for the family, with savings of 30 to 60 percent off suggested retail.

Fashions 4 Kids
Brand-name apparel and outerwear for girls and boys from infant sizes to size 14. Discounts are usually from 30 to 50 percent. This store serves as a girl's beauty pageant mecca. They carry Martha's Minatures, Sundi Pageant dresses, and accompanying accessories.

Fenn Wright & Mason
Fenn Wright & Mason, Basix, Career, and Intro updated casual and career apparel for men and women at 40 percent off department store prices.

Fieldcrest Cannon
Towels, kitchen linens, comforters, blankets, sheets, and more are available in a spectrum of colors. First-quality goods, closeouts, and imperfects, all at factory-direct savings of 40 to 60 percent. Pillows, mattress pads, shower curtains, and accessories for bed and bath are excellent values.

The Finish Line
Athletic shoes and apparel at outstanding prices. College logo apparel and accessories plus socks and shoe care products.

Flambeau
The Flambeau factory produces and its outlet sells plastic tackle boxes, fishing boxes and buckets, waterfowl and hunting decoys, Art-

bin storage containers, packing and storage systems, ProTech golf bags, and Duncan YoYos and toys. Goods range from first quality to irregulars, buy-outs, and seconds.

Florsheim

Choose from a large selection of dress, casual, and athletic shoes in sizes 6 to 15 and A to EEE widths. Direct from the factory savings on first-quality merchandise, closeouts, and irregulars are from 50 to 75 percent.

Footsaver Shoes

Ladies Footsaver and Barefoot Freedom shoes in a huge selection of styles and sizes. All shoes are made in the United States, mostly first quality with some irregulars. Outlet specializes in ladies' all-leather orthopedic shoes.

Fostoria

An assortment of first-quality and seconds stemware, giftware, tableware, and dinnerware direct from the manufacturer with savings from 50 to 75 percent.

14 Plus Pizazz

Though not a factory outlet, Bonnie & Bill, Chez, French Vanilla, and Barry Ashley brand-name women's fashions, in sizes 14 plus, are discounted every day. Mostly first-quality goods with some irregulars and seconds.

Fox River Glove

Leather work gloves and mittens from the factory with discounts up to 50 percent. Irregulars and overruns of Wigwam socks, Chic jeans, Spaulding jackets, dress gloves, and first-quality Minnetonka moccasins are sold at discount prices.

Fragrance World

World-famous men's and women's fragrances, cosmetics, and accessories, all at discounts of 20 to 60 percent off suggested retail prices.

Frontier Fruit & Nut Co.

Dried fruits, nuts, candies, meats, cheeses, and gifts shipped year-round. America's leading nut, dried fruit, and old-fashioned candy shop.

Frugal Fox Wallpaper
First-quality top-brand wall coverings, in stock or special order, discounted up to 50 percent or more. Blinds and shades at deep discounts, too. Designer assistance available.

Frugal Frank's
Brand-name shoes for the entire family with discounts from 20 to 40 percent off regular retail prices.

Fuller Brush
Save from 20 to 50 percent every day on famous Fuller Brush mops, brooms, brushes, chemicals, and personal care products. More than 82 years experience in supplying households with quality products allows Fuller Brush to extend a 100 percent satisfaction guarantee.

Full Size Fashion
Affordability and fashion go hand in hand to give the stylish edge to the full-figured woman.

Fureal Leathers
The Midwest's largest selection of men's and women's leathers, furs, and motorcycle garments at everyday savings of 50 to 75 percent. Big men's sizes to 60. Satisfaction guaranteed.

Gabel's Men's Wear
Jaymar-Ruby men's merchandise, Sansabelt slacks, sport coats, shirts, and sweaters are 30 to 50 percent off retail prices. Goods are all first quality.

Gant
Updated men's sportswear, featuring dress shirts, sports shirts, knits, rugbys, sweaters, and slacks.

GeGe's
Discounted apparel for women.

Gentlemen's Wear House
Manufacturer of men's American-made suits, sport coats, and slacks at 30 to 50 percent off. Some stores carry women's apparel.

Gentry Shop
The Gentry label is put into men's apparel from famous makers like Calvin Klein and Perry Ellis. The first-quality sportswear, suits, dress shirts, and ties are then discounted 30 to 40 percent. Tailoring available at additional cost.

The Genuine Article/OshKosh B'Gosh
Latest fashions in sportswear, at 20 to 50 percent off for the whole family. Sizes from infants to adults.

Gerber
Up to 60 percent off suggested retail is the savings offered at this factory-owned and -operated outlet. First-quality, seconds, and closeout Gerber nursers and accessories, oral development and feeding aids, safety products, toys, and Gerber clothing are stocked. Name-brand children's clothing in sizes infant through 14 plus baby furniture are available.

Gift Outlet
First-quality giftware and home decorating accessories featuring brass, crystal, porcelain, and more, all at 30 to 70 percent below retail prices.

Gilligan O'Malley
High-quality ladies' sleepwear, loungewear, and robes in alluring styles and colors direct from the manufacturer at 40 to 60 percent off.

Gitano
Savings of 20 to 50 percent, direct from the manufacturer, on casual and active sportswear for the whole family. Gloria Vanderbilt and E. J. Gitano are among the labels stocked in sizes for juniors, misses, maternity, plus sizes, men, and kids. Underwear, outerwear, socks, bodywear, and other accessories are available.

Gitano Children
Infants' and children's casual and active sportswear direct from the manufacturer with savings of 20 to 50 percent.

Gold Connection
Specializes in fine 14K-gold jewelry, custom design repair, fine estate jewelry, and silver and gold coins with discounts up to 75 percent.

Gold N Things
Gold, silver, and gemstones at discount prices. A wide selection of fashion and designer jewelry, sculpture, and gifts.

Graham Industries Home Furnishings
Factory-direct lamps and shades, furniture, wallpaper, bedding, and framed pictures are among the variety of goods offered. First-quality goods are discounted 25 percent. Seconds and irregulars are marked and sold at greater discounts. Lamp repair and lamp-shade recovering services are available.

Great Lakes Trading Company
A wide selection of active footwear, at factory-direct prices, for the entire family. You'll find the necessary gear for hiking, boating, running, and walking.

The Great Midwest Craftmarket
Affordable, handcrafted, first-quality gifts and accessories created in clay, metal, wood, fiber, paper, glass, and leather. Many one-of-a-kind pieces. Special year-round "Christmas Corner."

Grey Goose
Country collectible gift store.

Haeger Potteries
Factory owned and operated, high-quality ceramics such as lamps, vases, and decorating accessories are the outlet's product line. Most goods are first quality along with some irregulars. The outlet will ship merchandise free of charge anywhere in the United States.

Half Price Store
Department store quality merchandise at half the department store

price. First-quality factory overstocks of toys, shoes, domestics, housewares, and men's, women's, and children's clothing and accessories are discounted 50 percent.

Hanes Activewear

Choose from first-quality or slightly imperfect activewear for the whole family, direct from the manufacturer. Colorful sweats, knit tops, T-shirts, socks, and more are 100 percent guaranteed.

harvé benard

A wide selection of women's designer apparel, accessories, and men's furnishings, all up to 40 percent off. Stylish seasonal selections in most sizes.

Hathaway

Geoffrey Beene, Jack Nicklaus, Warners, Christian Dior, Olga, Thane, White Stag, Speedo, Chaps, Puritan, Hathaway, and Pringle are examples of the first-quality merchandise produced by this leading manufacturer's many divisions. Expect discounts from 30 to 60 percent off original price.

Head Factory Outlet

Men's and women's sporting apparel for all seasons discounted from 20 to 70 percent.

Helly-Hansen

Manufacturers of apparel, activewear, and accessories for cross-country and downhill skiing, biking, sailing, running, and other activities at 30 to 60 percent off.

Henson Lingerie/Henson-Kickernick

Quality Henson-Kickernick lingerie at savings of 45 to 75 percent direct from the manufacturer. Items include sleepwear, daywear, foundations, panties, and bras.

Herrschners

Premiere supplier of needlework, craft kits, and accessories offers goods to the public through its outlet store and factory. Outlet discounts are up to 50 percent. Factory store discounts discontinued merchandise 50 percent; catalog merchandise is at retail. Annual factory warehouse sale features savings of 50 to 80 percent.

Hickey-Freeman
Men's apparel direct from the manufacturer, discounted from 30 to 70 percent.

Hilda of Iceland
Save 30 to 70 percent on the finest woolen knits for the entire family. Sweaters, hats, capes, and more in that famous Icelandic look are sold directly from the manufacturer.

Hit or Miss
First-quality, current-season women's blazers, skirts, slacks, dresses, suits, and coordinating separates from brand-name manufacturers at 20 to 50 percent below department store prices.

Home Decor Outlet
Curtains, draperies, blankets, pillows, towels, sheets, bathroom, and kitchen accessories all at discount prices.

House of Large Sizes
Fashion specialist in women's large-size apparel, from size 14 and up, plus half sizes.

Houseware Outlet Store
A large assortment of Chef Craft gadgets, bakeware, and tumblers. Selections from Anchor, Ekco, Colonial Kitchen, Wixon spices, Sterilite, various microwave accessories, glassware, and candies. Fremware at 20 to 70 percent off.

Hush Puppies
See Little Red Shoe House.

I.B. Diffusions
Women's apparel and accessories at 30 to 70 percent off. Manufacturer's labels include I.B. Diffusion, I.B. Diffusion Sports, Santoria, Marc Allen, Joye & Fun, and Rediffusion.

Ideas
Women's career and casual apparel from the manufacturer. Ideas, Dreams, Wishes, and Grand Ideas labels are discounted from 30 to 40 percent off retail prices.

Indiana Glass
First-quality, irregular, and overstocked Indiana Glass and Colonial Glass comes straight from the factory. Prices start at nineteen cents. Glasses, pitchers, ashtrays, candlesticks, dishes, candles, and other household glassware is discounted 50 percent.

Izod Company Store
Factory direct to you, Izod/LaCoste fashions for men, women, and children at savings of 30 to 60 percent off manufacturer's suggested retail.

Izod/Ship 'n Shore/Monet
Direct from the manufacturer, high-quality fashions for men, women and children discounted from 30 to 50 percent off manufacturer's suggested retail prices.

J & S Liquidators
Solid oak reproduction cabinetry. Can be first quality, irregulars, or closeouts.

Jaymar/Jaymar-Ruby
Jaymar, Sansabelt, Racquet Club, and Lady Sansabelt fashions direct from the manufacturer at savings of 30 to 70 percent.

J. C. Penney Catalog Outlet
Penney catalog merchandise, overstocked or discontinued, is available at substantial savings. Look for men's, women's, and children's shoes and apparel, sporting goods, furniture, and domestic goods. New merchandise comes in daily. The selection is always different. Returned catalog merchandise, due to wrong color, size, or style, is also carried at the outlet. A few items with corrected mechanical or electrical defects, missing parts, or damages from shipment are also stocked. Check for specific warranty details at each outlet store.

J. C. Penney Furniture Warehouse
Furniture for all rooms of your house from Penney's Toledo warehouse. New, mostly canceled custom-ordered pieces with some damage and overstocked goods at savings from 40 to 70 percent off original price.

J. Crew
Super savings of 30 to 70 percent on classic apparel and sportswear for men and women direct from the manufacturer.

Jefferson Industries, Inc.
Discounts of 50 percent or more on brand-name carpet mats, room-size remnants, runners, accent rugs, and indoor/outdoor carpet direct from the manufacturer. Merchandise is irregular or seconds.

Jennings Decoy Company
Large selection of first-quality, direct-from-the-factory decorative wildlife gifts, decoys, and carving supplies. Customized orders are accepted.

Jersild
Knit goods for the entire family direct from the factory at wholesale prices. Merchandise includes first-quality goods as well as irregulars, closeouts, overruns, and one-of-a-kind samples. Wool throws, hats, mittens, scarves, and socks are also featured.

Jewelies
Huge assortment of custom jewelry for women discounted at 40 to 70 percent below regular retail prices. Similar savings are available on gift items, cards, watches, perfumes, clocks, key chains, scarves, and more.

J. G. Hook
Delightfully affordable prices on this top-quality manufacturer's classic sportswear, including coats and outerwear, for misses, petites, and women. Savings run from 30 to 70 percent.

J.H. Collectibles
For the fashion-conscious woman. Sportswear and separates in sizes 2 to 16 and a full line of petites at 30 to 60 percent off suggested retail prices.

Jindo Furs
Beautiful furs, shearlings, leathers, and suedes at great values. All sorts of outerwear, rainwear, and accessories round out the store's offerings.

J. Knitwear
Socks, underwear, hosiery, and sport accessories for men and women.

Johnston's Fashions for Children
Betti Terral, Fischel, and Petite Gamine children's apparel is discounted from 40 to 60 percent. A true manufacturer's outlet.

Jonathan Logan
Misses' and petite sizes famous-label career wear, dresses, activewear, suits, and outerwear. Famous brands, at savings of 30 to 70 percent, include Villager, R & K Kollection, Misty Harbor, Action Scene, and Rosemarie Reid. Jewelry by Lisner and Encore.

Jones NY
Save from 30 to 70 percent on top-quality women's suits and separates including Jones New York, Dior, Seville, and Jones Wear.

Jordache
This store has the look and prices, 30 to 60 percent off, on streetwear, accessories, and shoes for men, women, and children.

Joseph & Feiss
Men's suits, sport coats, slacks, shirts, ties, tuxedos, and sweaters direct from the manufacturer. Sizes range from 36 to 56 in short, short portly, regular, long, and extra-long for first-quality goods discounted from 45 to 60 percent off standard retail prices.

Julie's Jewelry
Value-priced unique custom jewelry and accessories.

Just About Perfect
Men's sportswear and accessories at a discount.

Just Kids
Direct from the factory, with savings of 20 to 60 percent. Quality children's name brands include Her Majesty, Cole for Kids, Camp Beverly Hills, and more.

Just My Size
Discounted name-brand Just My Size hosiery and lingerie, in sizes 38 to 52 or 1X to 5X, for the full-figured woman.

Just Pants
Hefty discounts from 30 to 70 percent on first-quality, irregular, and seconds young men's and women's tops and bottoms. Brand names include Levi, Guess, Ocean Pacific, and Jordache in a broad selection of models and sizes.

K & M Bed and Bath
Nationally advertised brands like Fieldcrest, West Point Pepperell, J. P. Stevens, and Cannon with super savings up to 50 percent. Sheets, comforters, bedspreads, towels, table linens, kitchen ensembles, wicker, pillows, and other items for the home.

Karoll's
First-quality men's merchandise, with some factory overruns, is consolidated from the company's nine Red Hanger Stores. Look for 20 to 60 percent average everyday savings on a great selection of brand-name fashions like Wrangler, Levi's, Manhattan, Botany 500, BVD, and more in regular and big and tall sizes.

Kelli's
Jewelry and giftware from top manufacturers like Seiko, Nao, Hummel, Fenton, Silver Deer, Cross, Pulsar, and many more with discounts ranging from 20 to 70 percent.

Kenneth Cole Shoes
First-quality men's and women's fashion footwear direct from the manufacturer with savings up to 50 percent. Tremendous savings on handbags and accessories.

Kids by Rainbow Fashions
Children's fashions from infant sizes and up. Gloves and accessories

for the family plus designer purses and luggage. Savings offered are up to 50 percent or more.

Kids Ca'pers
Discounted children's wear; girls from newborn to size 14, boys from newborn to size 7.

Kids Mart
Discounts of 20 to 50 percent on first-quality children's clothing and accessories by famous manufacturers such as OshKosh, Carters, Levi's, Lee, Buster Brown, and more. Gift certificates and gift boxes available.

KidsPort USA
The number-one brand of children's apparel, Health-Tex, comes direct from the manufacturer. Discounts run from 25 to 60 percent off suggested retail on sizes from infant to 14.

Kingsley Furniture
Makers of fine upholstered furniture for more than sixty years. Features traditional and French provincial upholstered living room pieces, mattress sets, tables, lamps, and fabrics by the yard.

Kitchen Collection
The widest selection of Wear-Ever cookware and Proctor-Silex appliances. This manufacturer's exclusive outlet offers discounts of 20 to 70 percent on first-quality, select manufacturer's seconds and closeout items.

Kitchen Place
More than 5,000 kitchen gadgets, houseware items, and gifts. Discounted are products from Ekco, Rubbermaid, Corning, Pyrex, and Longchamp crystal, to name a few.

Knits by K.T.
Current ladies' sweaters and knits by Kenneth Too plus sportswear by other famous makers are featured at this factory-owned-and-operated store. Misses' and large sizes are discounted from 25 to 60 percent off regular retail prices.

Kuppenheimer Men's Clothiers
Manufacturers of first-quality men's apparel that's sold exclusively in company-owned retail stores. Eliminates the middleman, passing on substantial savings (40 percent below competitive retail), to the customer.

LaCrosse Footwear, Inc.
Farm, work, industrial, and protective vinyl and rubber footwear and accessories. Rain and winter boots for the entire family from the Wisconsin manufacturer since 1897. Sporting, lightweight, and cold weather pacs, waders, and hip boots are also offered.

Lady Slipper Designs
A nonprofit cottage industry that sells to trendsetters like Bloomingdale's and Neiman Marcus. Discontinued and slightly flawed seconds in Victorian, Georgian, and Greek Revival style birdhouses; whimsical soft sculptures including an exquisite line of black velvet felines and Indian crafts are among items offered at substantial savings.

L.A. Lifestyles
Discounts from 30 to 70 percent off the complete line of the latest fashions for men, women, and teens.

Lamp and Shade Outlet
Hundreds of lamp shades in stock. Brass, crystal, wood, and stained-glass Tiffany-style lamps for dresser, desk, and floor. Ceiling fixtures and swags, too.

Lands' End Outlet/Combo/Not Quite Perfect Stores
First-quality, overstock, and end-of-season classic sportswear, dress shirts, dresses, children's wear, and domestics with a minimum savings of 20 percent off catalog prices. Not Quite Perfect stores carry items not considered first quality. Initially marked down 40 percent, items are regularly marked down to an additional 75 percent off the first 40 percent. Combo stores carry first-quality merchandise, overstocks, and discontinued items, marked with blue tags; and customer returns, marked with green tags.

Lazarus Final Clearance
Front Street level for clothing, sixth floor for furniture, domestics, and

housewares. End-of-season, first-quality merchandise from area Lazarus stores is marked down on a regular basis. Discounts start at 25 percent and go to 75 percent off the last ticketed price. Goods change daily.

The Leather Factory

The full leather store. Western boots, leather jackets, vests, purses, belts, and many more leather items are discounted from 25 to 75 percent every day.

Leather Loft

Luxury leather for less. Savings on handbags, luggage, briefcases, jackets, and designer accessories.

Leather Manor

Choose from a varied array of wallets, handbags, luggage, travel essentials, and briefcases. Save 15 to 70 percent on quality brands like Ashley-Moore, Carryland, Park Avenue, T. Capezi, and others. An exceptional selection of eelskin accessories and leather luggage is available.

Leggoons Sportswear

Upscale, cotton, active sportswear and beachwear in sizes from toddlers through adults extra-large. Direct from the manufacturer discounts run from 30 to 70 percent.

L'eggs/Hanes/Bali

Save 20 to 50 percent or more off suggested retail on slight imperfects, closeouts, and overstocks. Choose from famous-brand hosiery, lingerie, socks, underwear, activewear, and more.

Lehmann's Danish Bakery and Kringle

Award-winning Danish kringle, as featured by Neiman Marcus. Cream puffs, éclairs, napoleons, tortes, real whipped-cream pies, and donuts complete the taste-tempting selection.

Libbey Glass

Direct from the factory, Libbey glass tumblers, stemware, and glass accessory pieces—more than 1,500 items in stock. Also, L. E. Smith ware, dinnerware, scented candles, and kitchen accessories.

Linen Mill
Discounted table and kitchen linens, decorative pillows, throws, and casual rugs for the home from this quality manufacturer.

Linens 'n Things
A specialty linen store that features quality, name-brand merchandise from leading designers and manufacturers at 20 to 40 percent off regular retail prices.

Little Red Shoe House/Hush Puppies (Wolverine)
Owned and operated by Wolverine World Wide. Fashionable name-brand footwear for the whole family is discounted 20 to 50 percent off retail prices. Lines include Hush Puppies, Wolverine Boots, Town & Country women's shoes, Harbor Town, Brooks, Bates, Wimzees, and Rogue River. Frequent special values on the shoes America loves best.

Liz Claiborne
Discounted, first-quality wear-now styles in misses' and petite dresses. Substantial savings of up to 75 percent on women's sportswear, handbags, and accessories plus men's furnishings and sportswear.

London Fog
Owned and operated by the makers of the finest-quality rain outerwear, jackets, and coats for men and women. Look for 50 percent off regular retail prices. Men's and women's umbrellas, hats, scarves, sweaters, and other articles are offered at substantial savings.

Loomcraft Home Decorating Fabrics
The Midwest's largest selection of home decorating fabrics. Thousands of bolts in stock. Kirsch drapery hardware, upholstery, drapery supplies, and foam are also discounted.

Mackintosh of New England
Direct from their New England factories is a large selection of women's pure wool Mackintosh coats. First-quality coats, slight irregulars, and samples are offered in missy, petite, and women's sizes. Their large selection of suits, separates, and two-piece dresses is also priced way below retail.

Made In Italy
The largest distributor of Capodimonte porcelain, Italian jewelry, leather goods, and alabaster.

Madison's Grand Finale
Savings up to 75 percent on women's apparel and accessories from brand-name manufacturers. Sent to the Grand Finale clearance outlet at the end of each season, the first-quality merchandise is consolidated from Madison's twenty-three stores.

Maidenform
Save up to 60 percent on Maidenform first-quality discontinued and closeout bras, panties, camisoles, half slips, sleepwear, daywear, garter belts, and lingerie.

Manhattan
First-quality, name-brand apparel for men and women with factory-direct savings of up to 60 percent off retail. Women's brands include Anne Klein, Manhattan, and Lady Arrow, some in plus and petite sizes. Featured men's brands include Manhattan, Perry Ellis, and John Henry.

Masters Fashion Center
A one-stop source for clothing for your entire family—infants' through large sizes. First-quality, buy-out, and seconds-type goods are discounted from 20 to 40 percent.

Maternity Wearhouse
First-quality complete line for the mother-to-be discounted from 15 to 50 percent below manufacturer's suggested retail. Expect to find casual, career wear, active, and after-five outfits, including lingerie.

Mattress Factory
The full line of mattresses and futon products is available to the public direct from the manufacturer at 10 percent over wholesale.

Maus Jewelry Imports
Price guarantees on rings with precious stones. Bargains on a vast array of 14K-gold and sterling silver jewelry.

Men's Clothing Outlet
American-made, first-quality goods, overruns, and cancellations in traditionally styled men's suits, sport coats, and slacks. Discounts are at least 50 percent off retail prices. Manufacturers' labels are removed.

Meystel/Rayco
First-quality and irregular merchandise and buy-outs of branded designer apparel for men, women, and children with discounts of 30 to 70 percent. In business since 1925, customers learn of the store through word of mouth as it does not advertise.

Mid America Shoes
Brand-name athletic, dress, and casual shoes for the entire family. Top of the line work boots.

Middleton Doll
The finest award-winning, artist-original porcelain and vinyl dolls direct from the factory with savings of 50 percent or more.

Midway Leather
Discounted leather apparel and accessories.

Midwestern Sports Togs/Berlin Glove Company
Deerskin gloves, garments, handbags, footwear, and accessories are available at the factory-owned and -operated outlet. Firsts, closeouts, and factory seconds are discounted from 30 to 50 percent. Custom tanning and tailoring of deerskins is available.

Midwest Glass & China
Savings up to 50 percent on glassware and china.

Mikasa
The factory-direct outlet features a vast selection of dinnerware, stemware, flatware, table linens, giftware, cookware, and more. Save up to 80 percent.

Milbern Clothing Co.
First-quality, in-season tailored clothing for the male or female professional. Suits, sport coats, pants, and more from manufacturers like

Palm Beach, Oleg Cassini, and Christian Brooks plus private label merchandise are sold at 20 to 50 percent off retail prices. Alterations available at cost.

Mill City

Lee jeans for the entire family in basic and fashionable styles. Lord Isaacs slacks. Current junior and updated missy looks in tops and outerwear.

Minnetonka

Savings from 25 to 75 percent off retail prices for this manufacturer's line of leading fragrances and luxury bath products. Goods are overruns, discontinued items, and production seconds. A selection of gift items is also available.

Mitchell Leather Shop

Save up to 60 percent on the latest Samsonite, Skyway, and other quality brands luggage, briefcases, and attaché cases. Outlet features leather handbags manufactured in Milwaukee.

Monterey Mills

The country's largest selection of deep-pile fur fabrics in first quality, closeouts, overruns, discontinued styles, and substandard items, direct from the mill. Savings are usually 50 percent. Remnants and scrap pieces are available by the pound. Goods available through the mail. A sample of each style and color in the product line is $4.00.

Montgomery Ward Clearance

Discontinued, reconditioned, and scratched/dented Montgomery Ward major appliances, furniture, electronics, and lawn and garden equipment are substantially discounted.

Multiples

Save from 40 to 60 percent off department store prices on Multiples modular "mix and match" knit apparel. First quality, easy care, no-iron, one size fits all in women's, plus, and children's sizes.

Munsingwear

First-quality menswear such as underwear, sport shirts, and pajamas at savings from 30 to 75 percent. Some outlets carry Vassarette intimate apparel.

Mushroom Shoes
Stylish, comfortable women's shoes like Cobbies, Mushrooms, Red Cross, and Selby come to you at great discounted prices.

Music Vision
Extensive selection of 45s, LPs, cassettes, compact discs, recording tapes, record care products, carrying cases, and posters. Look over the large budget section of records and tapes. Discount prices all the time.

Native Wood Products
Direct from the factory, a selection of seconds and overstocks of woodenware kitchen, bath, and home accessories. Prices are a fraction over wholesale.

Nettle Creek
First-quality, current-season bedspreads, decorator pillows, fabric by the yard, and custom-made window dressings are 35 percent off retail prices. First-quality items can be discounted up to 60 percent. A special clearance section offers discounts to 70 percent for irregular merchandise. Accessories like dust ruffles, pillow shams, upholstered headboards, and boudoir furniture are available or can be custom ordered.

New England Classics
Direct from the manufacturer at 40 percent off regular retail, first-quality sweaters, tops, and coordinates for women in all-natural fibers.

Newport Sportswear/Newport for Men
Current-season, first-quality men's coordinated sportswear, shirts, sweaters, outerwear, and activewear are discounted 35 percent.

New Visions
Sunglasses, reading glasses, sports glasses, and all-weather glasses all at a discount. Accessories featured include cords, cases, and clip-on glasses.

Nickels
Women's shoes and accessories.

Nike
A superb selection of athletic footwear, apparel, and accessories from the manufacturer with discounts from 30 to 50 percent.

Nilani
Nilani and Billy Jack brands of dresses, blouses, knitwear, and sportswear with manufacturer discounts from 20 to 50 percent. Sizes available for missy, petite, and large sizes.

Ninth Street Bridal and Formal Outlet
Name-brand gowns for brides, attendants, mothers of the bride and groom, plus gowns for proms, pageants, and other social occasions. Savings are up to 70 percent on buy-outs, samples, and liquidations. Everything is off the rack, no orders. Lingerie, invitations, and accessories are also available.

No Nonsense
Family hosiery and sportswear.

Nu-Look Fashions
Men's suits, topcoats, and sport coats at substantial discounts in sizes 36 to 54. All items on the rack are first quality. Direct from the manufacturer that supplies Penney's and Federated department stores.

Old Mill Ladies Sportswear
Updated ladies sportswear in coordinates and contemporary separates, dresses, and suits. Sizes range from 4 to 18 and petite sizes 4 to 16. The exclusive factory outlet carries Country Suburbans, Handmacher, Suburban Petites, and Weathervane Petites with savings from 25 to 70 percent.

Old Time Pottery
An ever-changing variety of wicker baskets, silk flowers and arrangements, crafts, lamps, pictures, and pottery. Famous brand-name din-

nerware, crystal, cookware, bakeware, and more, all at tremendous savings.

Oneida
Super savings ranging from 20 to 70 percent direct from the manufacturer of stainless and silverplated flatware, silverplated holloware, items for children and babies plus a large selection of gifts.

Oops We Goofed
The source for first-quality window coverings. Tremendous savings of 50 to 80 percent off retail prices on Graber drapery hardware and vertical blinds, Bali micro/mini blinds, custom draperies and valances, custom quilted bedspreads, and upholstery fabrics.

OshKosh B'Gosh
See The Genuine Article.

The Paint and Wallpaper Factory Outlet
Nationally advertised name-brand paints at discount prices.

The Paper Factory
Party goods, decorations, gift wrap, bows, ribbons, greeting cards, books, games, puzzles, and paper office supplies, all under one roof, plus savings up to 50 percent.

Paul Revere
First-quality items, overstocks, and seconds on a variety of Revere Ware at up to 50 percent off retail. All stores do not have all merchandise.

Perfume Boutique
Expect a large selection of classic men's and women's fragrance reproductions at 85 percent savings plus balms, lotions, and atomizers.

Pfaltzgraff Collector's Center
The largest selection of stoneware in America at 10 to 50 percent off retail prices. Save on stoneware, glassware, kitchen gadgets, decorative accessories, linens, and housewares. Special prices on Pfaltzgraff collectibles.

Pickard China

The only Pickard China factory outlet, selling only company-manufactured dinnerware and giftware. Blemish-free seconds run from 40 to 60 percent off comparable retail prices. Decorative accessories are made exclusively for the outlet store. Occasionally, factory close-outs are stocked.

Pilgrim Glass/Pilgrim Silks

Direct from the factory silk flowers, Pilgrim Glass, handblown decorative glass vases, baskets, and brass with savings from 50 to 60 percent.

Plumm's

In-season, first-quality styles for misses and juniors are 20 to 50 percent off everyday comparable prices. Stylish, affordable clothes for work, evenings, or weekends.

Plums Sweaters for Less

Sweaters, sweaters, sweaters for the entire family. Out-of-season, first-quality and slightly flawed irregulars consolidated from Winona Knits outlets are featured with discounts from 30 to 70 percent.

Polly Flinders

Quality hand-smocked girls' dresses in sizes from newborn to 14. Matching hairbows, tights, and panties are available to complement an outfit. Some stores carry boys' sizes 4 months to 4T.

Polo/Ralph Lauren

Fine designer men's, women's, and boys' clothing, home furnishings, leather accessories, and fragrances with savings from 20 to 50 percent.

Pottery and More

Low, everyday prices for housewares, domestics, crafts, and gifts.

Prestige Fragrance & Cosmetics, Inc.

Savings of 25 to 70 percent off suggested retail value on world-famous brand-name men's and women's fragrances, toiletries, and cosmetics.

Prevue Fashions

More than 1,000 missy, junior, petite, large, and half-size dresses in stock. Discounted prices of 40 to 60 percent off retail prices on name-brand dresses and coordinate groups. Savings on jeans, leisurewear, sportswear, knits, career and dress suits, separates, and outerwear.

Publishers Outlet
An assortment of coffee-table–type gift and children's books, mostly hard cover. All are first-quality overruns, with discounts of at least 30 percent off list price.

Purdy Products, Inc.—Milwaukee Soap Company
An outlet store that offers discounts from 10 to 50 percent on first-quality janitorial products. Among the goods available are brooms; mops; dishwashing, laundry, and hand soaps; pails; floor care and paper products.

Rainbow Fashions
Juniors and misses can be the belle of the ball and save from 20 to 70 percent below retail on first-quality famous-designer fashions such as Ocean Pacific, Hang Ten, OOPS, and Forenza.

Rainbow Sunglasses
The newest styles in quality sunglasses at discount prices.

Rainbow Times
Watches, clocks, alarms, and novelties at outlet prices.

Rawlings
"The Mark of a Pro." For the sportsminded, NFL-licensed apparel and equipment plus Rawlings sports equipment and clothing are available at 40 to 60 percent off suggested retail prices.

Reading Bag
Save up to 60 percent every day on thousands of name-brand handbags, wallets, luggage, and business cases.

Reading Shoes
Save 25 percent or more on full-grain leather Bass footwear like Weejuns, Bucs, Sunjuns sandals, and other classic footwear and accessories.

Recie's Sample Shop
More than eighty lines of salesmen's samples with discounts from 30 to 50 percent less than retail prices. Among the many brands offered, you'll discover Jones New York, Breckenridge, J. H. Collectibles, Jantzen, Karen Kane, and many more.

Regal
Factory-direct housewares, cookware, and kitchen appliances featuring savings of 30 to 70 percent. It's all here: Regal Ware stainless steel, cast-aluminum and drawn-aluminum range-top cookware; microwave ovenware and accessories; food processors, electric knives, juicers, coffee makers, and corn poppers; vacuum cleaners and air cleaners. Good value on seconds, closeouts, and overruns when available.

Regal Rugs
Quality workmanship and attractive designs are available direct from this manufacturer of handcrafted rugs. A complete line of basic and designer rugs, even for large areas, plus towels at prices a minimum of 50 to 70 percent off retail. Rugs are irregular or closeouts because they are a shade off the called-for color criteria, which in no way affects wear.

The Ribbon Outlet, Inc.
More than 3,000 varieties of first-quality ribbons and trims in precut lengths, bulk spools, or cut by the yard to your dimensions. Distinctive handcrafted gift items, craft supplies, novelties, and seasonal items are sold by sewing-astute sales associates at discounts of 20 to 70 percent.

Richmond Brothers
Men's and women's coats and suits from the manufacturer with discounts up to 40 percent.

Rosewood Galleries
First-quality artwork for the home, including custom framing. Discounts on brand names like Hargrove, Carson, Perez, Cooper, Russell, Cox, Lee, and many more run from 25 to 40 percent.

Royal Belgian Rug
Excellent quality floor coverings for less.

Royal Doulton

Fine china and crystal from a premier manufacturer. Merchandise includes Royal Doulton, Royal Albert, Minton, Bunnykins, Beatrix Potter, and character and Toby mugs with discounts from 20 to 70 percent. A bridal registry and a collector's club are added services.

Royal Robbins

Casual clothing for men and women with outdoor spirit. Owned and operated by the manufacturer, the outlet's discounts range from 35 to 75 percent.

Ruff Hewn

Rugged, comfortable sportswear for men and women who lead an active life-style at savings of 35 to 50 percent.

Russell/Jerzees

Family sports apparel at 30 to 50 percent off retail prices.

Rybicki's Cheese Store

Fresh from the factory, more than fifty varieties of Rybicki cheese at 20 percent less than retail. Fresh cheese curds are available daily plus wine, sausage, beer, and gifts.

Salem China

A wide selection of American-made merchandise direct from the manufacturer: L. A. Smith handmade crystal, Salem china, Sadler English teapots, Company 2000, Mikasa, and more.

S & K Famous Brand Men's Wear

Famous-brand men's suits include Austin Reed, Hart, Schaffner & Marx, Lord and Taylor, and many more. Also men's slacks, shirts, ties, and accessories.

Sans Souci Lingerie

Fine-quality workmanship and materials go into this moderately priced line of lingerie that is discounted from 40 to 60 percent.

Sassafras

Housewares, gifts, and contemporary life-style products for adults and children at savings of 10 to 50 percent.

Scents and Soaps
Fragrances and gift soaps.

Schuette
Mirror first-quality and irregular cookware and bakeware. Foley Mills, West Bend, and Empire electric appliances, Nesco roasters, and cookbooks are all brought to you at factory-direct prices.

Sears Outlet/Surplus
Savings of 20 to 70 percent off most original catalog and retail prices every day. Merchandise for home and family including clothing, housewares, electronics, furniture, and more.

Sequels Book Outlet
Publisher closeouts discounted 50 percent or more. Selections include children's, fiction, cooking, travel, and a variety of others. Something for everyone.

70% Off
Just as the name indicates, discounts are up to 70 percent off brand-name fashions and accessories for men, women, and children.

Shapely
Classic Leslie Fay blouses, dresses, knitwear, and sportswear in a range of sizes including petite and plus at savings of 30 to 50 percent.

Shapes Activewear
A full line of activewear, sportswear, pants, tops, sweatshirts, leotards, tights, hosiery, leg warmers, socks, ballet shoes, and accessories from the famous American manufacturer with discounts of 20 to 50 percent.

Sherwood Coats of Ohio
Direct from the factory in Alliance, Ohio, first-quality and irregular ladies' outerwear is sold with a minimum savings of 40 percent.

Shoe Cents
First-quality brand-name buy-outs from major department stores. Women's athletics and boots and men's shoes are $40 or less; women's dress and casual shoes are $20 or less.

Shoe Factory Clearance Center
Fantastic savings on brand-name shoes for the entire family. Nearly 10,000 pairs, all priced at $19.88 or less.

Shoe Manufacturers Outlet
"The best brands at the best price." Shoes for the entire family. All sizes available plus special orders.

Shoes by Lara
Deep discounts every day of 20 to 50 percent on first-quality women's shoes, boots, and handbags. Well-known brand names include 9 West, Truffles, Faragola, Bruno Valenti, and more.

Shoe Sensation
Where you'll find shoe values for the entire family. Top leading brands in a large selection of styles.

Shoe Stop
Discounted first-quality and buy-out ladies' designer shoes featuring name brands such as Aigner, Van Eli, Naturalizer, Enzo, and more in sizes 4 to 12.

Silk Greenhouse
Silk flowers, by the stem or in designer arrangements, substantially discounted. Also offered are decorator containers, dried flowers, wedding and shower items, craft accessories, holiday ornaments, and accessories to beautify the home.

Simandl Coats
This manufacturer of first-quality, pure wool ladies' coats offers discounts up to 60 percent off retail prices right at the factory. Hundreds of coats stocked. Can custom-make coats from any style or fabric in stock to any sleeve or length.

Sizes Unlimited
First-quality apparel for the fuller-figure woman in sizes 14 to 32.

Skyr
Skyr and Catcher sweaters, turtlenecks, and coordinated sportswear at 40 percent off retail prices.

Slightly Imperfix

Returned goods from a major catalog/retail store are 50 percent off catalog prices. Drapes and bedspreads, 50 percent off J. C. Penney sales prices. Vinyl-clad particleboard furniture is available as discontinued or buy-out merchandise.

Smoler Brothers Fashion

Direct from the manufacturer, with labels removed, are better ladies' fashions. Savings start at 20 percent for first-quality items. Samples, seconds, closeouts, test runs, and discontinued and end-of-season merchandise can be discounted up to 50 percent.

Sneakers-n-Cleats

Sporting goods, athletic shoes, and accessories for men and women.

Socks Galore/Socks Galore & More

A sock-lover's dream come true. More than 60,000 pairs of designer dress, sport, tube, and slouch socks for the entire family priced at 25 to 80 percent off retail. Brand names include Anne Klein, Christian Dior, Camp, Hue, and more.

Specials—Exclusively Levi Strauss & Co.

Levi Strauss & Co. fashions for men, women, and children. Dockers, 501s, women's 900 series, jean jackets, and much more are 50 percent off the ticketed price.

Sports Factory

Licensed college and major-league team logo sports apparel.

Sportsland USA

Sports souvenirs and apparel.

Sports Wearhouse

Family athletic clothing with discounts from 30 to 60 percent. Logo sweats of ABA, NFL, NCAA, NHL, colleges, and Disney characters. Brand names like Chalk Line, McGregor, OP, and O'Neill.

Stone Mountain Handbags

Top-quality leather goods' manufacturer of Stone Mountain, Saddle River, and Ande lines; discounts on handbags, travel bags, and accessories from 20 to 70 percent.

Swank

Extensive selection of men's and women's jewelry, personal leather goods, belts, fragrances, gifts, and personal accessory items. Lines include Swank, Pierre Cardin, Alexander Julian, Royal Copenhagen, Anne Klein, and Richard Scott at 40 to 70 percent off.

Sweat Graphics

Factory-direct prices from 20 to 30 percent off suggested retail on top-quality, high-fashion, hand-painted outfits and skylines of Chicago. Originals at a low price.

Sweats, Etc.

This unisex sportswear shop is the newest division of Casual Male. Featured are fleece sweat pants and tops in colors, colors, and more colors.

The Sweatshirt Company

Family apparel and activewear priced from 30 to 40 percent off. Mix and match styles and colors. Sizes for the whole family including big and tall for men and plus sizes for women.

Swiss Miss

First-quality embroidered fabrics and laces suited for bridal and fine formal apparel available directly from the factory. Discounts range from 20 to 50 percent.

Sycamore

Women's moderate casual apparel with well-known labels like Bill Blass jeans, My Michele, Options, Signet dresses, and more, always at a discount.

Sylvester's Fashion Outlet

Top-brand children's fashions priced at 50 to 80 percent off retail. Clothing from manufacturers that line department-store racks like Guess, Carters, Healthtex, and OshKosh.

Tanner

Dresses, sportswear, casual wear, and activewear for women at this factory-owned and -operated store. Look for discounts of 30 to 75 percent on Tanner, Tanner Sport, Doncaster, and Tanner Country labels.

Tempo Fashions

Quality women's fashions with brand names like Villager, Jordache, Scarlett Borelli, and more are available every day at deep discounts from 50 to 70 percent.

Temptations Jewelry

Designer pieces to everyday wear in fine jewelry, 14K gold, sterling silver, and marcasite. A full line of accessories: scarves, belts, handbags, and sunglasses to complement your wardrobe.

That's Our Bag

Handbags, briefcases, luggage, and accessories at incredibly low prices.

This Gift's For You

Cardinals and Anheuser-Busch name brands on T-shirts, jackets, steins, etc. with savings up to 60 percent.

Thorngate Ltd. Slack Outlet

A division of Hart, Schaffner & Marx. This outlet carries imperfect, name-brand, American-made men's dress and casual slacks plus some shirts.

Ties, Etc.

Save 50 percent or more on a large selection of quality neckwear. You'll recognize famous brands like Givenchy, Liberty, and Brown & Church. Headquarters for hard-to-find extra-long ties, clip-on ties, bow ties, and boys' ties, plus belts and suspenders.

Tiffany Lamp

"Tiffany Style" hand-leaded stained-glass lamps are discounted up to 40 percent.

Todd's

Largest selection of men's, women's, and children's first-quality Western and work boots in the Chicago area. Expect discounts from 20 to 50 percent and a wide variety of harder-to-find sizes and widths.

Tool Warehouse

Great buys on hand tools of every description for the home, car, shop, garden, or farm. Hundreds of quality tools to choose from, all at truckload prices.

Top of the Line Cosmetics
Save on designer and brand-name cosmetics and fragrances from 25 to 75 percent off retail. Gift sets, makeup brushes, skin care products, and travel bags are also part of the large inventory. Trained consultants also provide color analysis and makeup advice.

totes/Sunglass World
The weather protection experts save you 50 to 75 percent off umbrellas, raincoats, rain hats, folding luggage, rubber boots, and more. Some outlets have travel accessories and a large selection of sunglasses when the Sunglass World section is included. All outlets feature overstocks, closeouts, and select irregulars.

Towel Factory Outlet Center
Linens, towels, sheets, and other items for bed and bath at low, low prices. Expect to find a mix of first-quality, second, irregular, and buyout goods from manufacturers like Cannon, Martex, St. Mary's, J. P. Stevens, and Royal Pacific.

Toy King
Discounted prices on nationally advertised toys. Shelves are stocked with child-pleasing items from Nintendo, Fisher-Price, Mattel, Kenner, Little Tykes, Parker Brothers, and many more.

Toy Liquidators
A wide selection of name-brand toys like Hasbro, Fisher-Price, Mattel, Playskool, and more, discounted up to 70 percent off suggested retail prices. Many are overstocks, package changes, and discontinued items. Some are sold at less than manufacturers' original wholesale prices.

Toys Unlimited
New goods arrive daily at this discounter of nationally advertised, top-quality, name-brand toys. Savings can be as high as 75 percent off retail prices.

TrendSetter Footwear
First-quality shoes like Hush Puppies, Town & Country, Brooks, and L. A. Gear come direct from the manufacturer, Wolverine Worldwide.

All shoes are priced 25 percent off retail with a full range of sizes and widths.

Trinkets 'n Treasures
Accessories to make every outfit a knockout. By-the-inch gold chains, custom-made to your specifications, come with lifetime guarantees.

Trophy Nut Store
In front of the 85,000-square-foot nut factory, nut products, mixes, and candies are sold in bulk or in one-pound packages at prices considerably less than retail.

The Ultimate Outlet
Irregular and samples of brand-name and designer apparel. Discounts range from 50 to 75 percent off suggested retail prices for current season fashions for men and women in sample sizes. There's also a smattering of shoes, purses, and accessories as well as a limited children's selection.

Underwriters Sales Outlet
Anything and everything under the sun. Inventory changes daily. Merchandise is 90 percent first quality with some seconds, irregulars, and buy-outs. Expect discounts from 30 to 80 percent off retail. Get here early. Customers begin lining up one hour prior to the 10:00 A.M. opening.

USCO
Casual sportswear and shoes at everyday discounts of 20 percent. Dexter, Keds, Converse, and Grasshoppers for the entire family. Clothing carries brand names like Wrangler, Devon, Maybelle, Misty Harbor, Career Club, Tamarack (jackets), Hanes, and more.

Value Center
A variety of first-quality and slightly irregular family sportswear and outerwear is discounted from 30 to 70 percent off manufacturers' suggested retail. Levi, Lee, Cotler, Jordache, JouJou, Esprit, Union Bay, and London Fog are among the many famous brand names available.

Van Heusen
First-quality, current-season men's and women's fashion apparel from the manufacturer at value prices. Savings of 20 to 60 percent on Van Heusen, Geoffrey Beene, Lady Van Heusen, and Aigner.

Vassarette

Women's lingerie in a variety of styles and colors sized to fit all figures. Bras, girdles, slips, camisoles, sleepwear, and more with discounts from 30 to 50 percent off the manufacturers' suggested retail price.

Vermillion

Quality ceramic housewares and wood furniture for your home, direct from the factory.

VF

From America's largest apparel manufacturer comes first-quality Lee jeans, Jantzen swimwear, Vanity Fair lingerie and sleepwear, Heron Cove Casuals, Kay Windsor dresses, and Bassett-Walker fleecewear for the entire family, all at 50 percent off the ticketed price. Irregulars are ticketed and save you even more.

Village Clock Shop

Grandfather, wall, and mantel clocks, all first quality from noted manufacturers like Ridgeway, Howard Miller, and Sligh. Discounts are from 30 to 50 percent. Pulaski Furniture curios and accent pieces are also stocked. Free statewide delivery and shipping nationwide.

Villeroy & Boch

Fine china, dinnerware, flatware, gourmet-ware, crystal, and giftware with the Villeroy & Boch, Wilkens, Asta, and Gallo brands discounted from 35 to 70 percent.

Waccamaw Pottery

Hard-to-beat discount prices on a tremendous selection of dinnerware, housewares, dried and silk flowers (loose or in arrangements), craft items, and so much more. Goods are all first quality with name brands like Mikasa, Libbey, Corning, and others. Discounts can be as much as 80 percent off department-store prices.

Wallet Works

First-quality leather wallets, clothes, key cases, and accessories are direct from the manufacturer. Find brand names like Stone Mountain, East Pak, High Sierra, and Desa plus briefcases, luggage, handbags, and travel gifts, all at savings of 25 to 75 percent.

Warehouse of Leathers

First-quality men's and women's leather apparel and accessories. Expect discounts of 10 to 20 percent below suggested retail price. Look for jackets, coats, pants, skirts, and a selection of eelskin accessories. Special purchases and sale items can make discounts soar to 50 percent or more.

Warnaco-Olga/Warner's

Famous-label, first-quality men's and women's apparel at 30 to 70 percent off. Look for Hathaway, Puritan, Thane, Dior, Chaps by Ralph Lauren, White Stag, Speedo, Olga, Warner's, and more.

Warren Cheese Plant

The creators of Apple Jack cheese. Their specialty is ethnic cheeses like Swiss, string, mozzarella, provolone, and others sold to wholesale restaurant and grocery accounts. Prices are considerably less than retail.

Watches-N-Stuff

More than 150 styles in fashion look-alike watches for men and women. These copycats mimic the look of Rolex, Gucci, and Seiko and are guaranteed for one year. You'll also find the Lorus line of Mickey Mouse watches. A one-stop shop for watch needs, they sell watchbands, straps, and accessories as well as watch batteries (installation included).

Wayside Workshop

Fine reproduction furniture and unique gifts. Unfinished furniture, woodenware, and gift items are also featured.

The Wear House

Samples, seconds, overruns, and damaged children's outerwear, sweaters, swimwear, and sportswear direct from an international manufacturer. Sizes range from infants' through size 14. Merchandise is usually from 30 to 50 percent off retail. All sales are final, and the policy is cash only.

Welcome Home

The store that makes your home beautiful. Featured brand names include Marion Yu, Country Lace, and Lasting Impressions. Choose from a wide selection of giftware, framed art, table linens and textiles, romantic lace items, fragrant scents for the home, dolls, candles, and more.

Wemco

A fantastic selection of men's brand-name neckwear and classic sportswear like Resilio, Wembley, Je Suis, and Lord Ascot. Sportswear is from 40 to 60 percent off, and neckwear is discounted from 60 to 80 percent.

West Bend

Complete line of the manufacturer's electrical appliances, coffee makers, fitness equipment, and more. Seconds, closeouts, and demonstrators that save you up to 50 percent.

West Point Pepperell

Linens, apparel, and home decorating accessories with brand names like Attelier, J. P. Stevens, Mar-Tex, Lady Pepperell, Utica, and Esprit. Savings range from 20 to 70 percent.

Westport, Ltd.

"Fashion . . . factory-to-you!" Top-quality labels including Westport, Ltd., Princeton Club, Atrium, and Milano for the career woman. Shop from the large collection of suits, dresses, sportswear, and separates in sizes 4 to 14.

What A Deal

Everything is $10 every day on new, name-brand women's clothing in juniors', missy, petite, and plus sizes.

Whistling Wings

The world's largest mallard duck hatchery offers fresh, frozen, and smoked mallards, quail, pheasant, turkey, and other wild game. Their products are found in the finest restaurants, gourmet food shops, and upscale stores like Neiman Marcus and Marshall Fields. Prices are about 50 percent off retail.

Whitewater Gloves

Ski, casual, dress, work, and hunting gloves. Jeans, belts, and jackets are also featured.

Windsor Shirt
The better way to buy a better shirt. From the manufacturer to you, more than 20,000 discounted men's dress and sports shirts in forty-eight sizes.

Winona Glove Sales
Dress and work gloves, purses, wallets, ski accessories, woolen caps, scarves, socks, and moccasins at savings of 50 percent and more.

Winona Knits
Sweaters, sweaters, and more sweaters in cotton, acrylic, wool, and wool blends for men, women, and children. High-quality American-made sweaters that are guaranteed.

Wooden Bench
Country gifts and furniture.

Woolen Mill
See Faribo Woolens Factory Store.

The Wool Shed
One-hundred-percent-natural yarn sportswear for men and women, spinning and weaving supplies, sheepskin items and gifts.

World Bazaar
International importers of casual home furnishings, accessories, and gifts, specializing in wicker and rattan. A large selection at warehouse prices.

Your Toy Center
Fisher-Price, Mattel, Coleco, Playskool, Milton Bradley, Matchbox, and other name-brand toys and games are discounted every day.

ILLINOIS

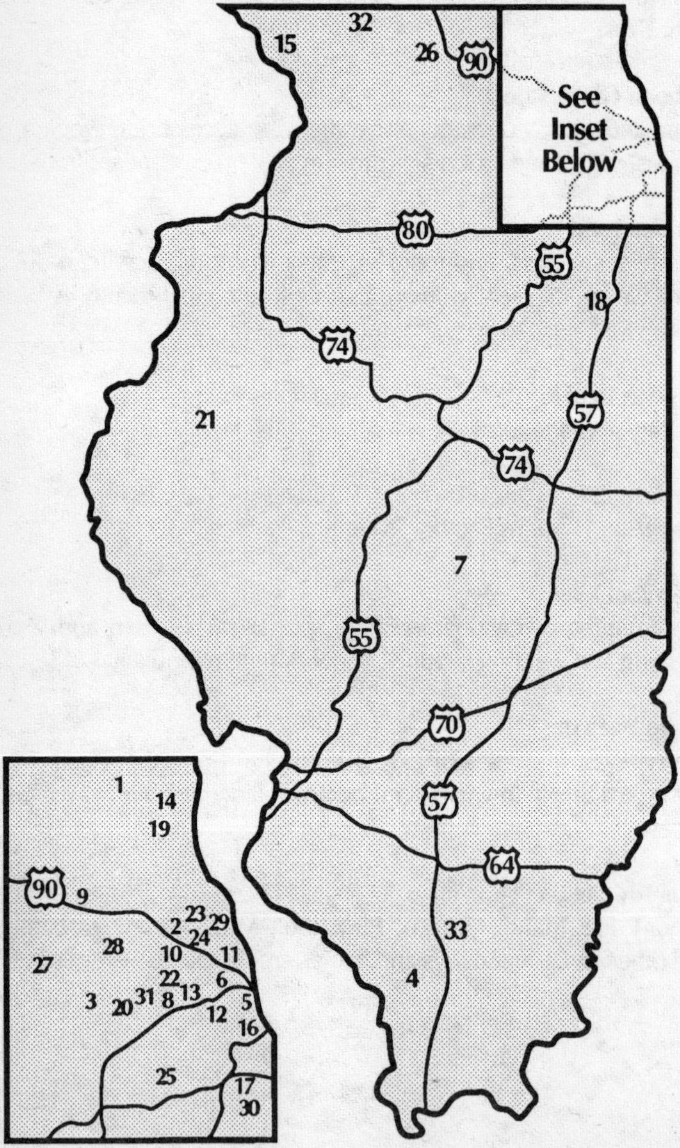
32
15
26
90
See Inset Below
80
55
18
74
57
21
74
7
55
70
57
64
33
4
1
14
19
90
9
23
29
2
24
28
10
11
27
22
6
3
20
31
8
13
5
12
16
25
17
30

ILLINOIS

Numbers to the left of entries in this legend correspond to the numbers on the accompanying map. The number to the right of each city's or town's name is the page number on which that municipality's outlets first appear.

ANTIOCH

Pickard China
782 Corona Avenue

Directions: I–94 to Rosecrans Road, exit west (Route 173); proceed 6 miles to Route 83 and turn right; continue to Depot Street and turn right, then left, at the next intersection (Corona Avenue); go round the bend and park in front of the Pickard Building.
Phone: (708) 395–3800
Hours: 8:30 A.M.–4:00 P.M., Monday–Friday
Additional Savings: Seasonal and holiday sales plus monthly specials
Credit Cards: Discover, MasterCard, Visa
Personal Checks: Yes; checks must be imprinted with name, address, and phone number.
Handicapped Accessible: Yes
Food: Nearly twenty fast-food stores and restaurants within a 2-mile radius
Bus Tours: Yes
Notes or Attractions: Display of hand-painted china created by Pickard craftsmen from 1893 to 1930 and sample of dinner service currently made for *Air Force One,* embassies, and other governmental/military agencies

ARLINGTON HEIGHTS

Burlington Coat Factory
Arlington Plaza

Directions: West Rand Road near Palantine Road
Phone: (312) 577–7878
Hours: 10:00 A.M.–9:00 P.M., Monday–Friday; 10:00 A.M.–6:00 P.M., Saturday; 11:00 A.M.–5:00 P.M., Sunday
Credit Cards: MasterCard, Visa

Personal Checks: Yes, with proper identification
Handicapped Accessible: Yes
Food: Available in the immediate area
Bus Tours: Yes

AURORA

Arbetman Brothers & Blaire
42 W. New York Street

Directions: I–88 to Route 31 south; proceed to Galena Boulevard. Turn left on Galena, traveling 2 blocks to Stolp Avenue; then turn left—parking available at North Island Center on Stolp Avenue. Walk 1 block north to New York Street and turn left. Store is 2 blocks to the west.
Phone: (708) 892–1828
Hours: Call ahead.
Credit Cards: MasterCard, Visa
Personal Checks: Yes, with proper identification
Handicapped Accessible: Yes
Bus Tours: Yes, parking at North Island Center lot on Stolp Avenue.

El-Bee Shoe Outlet
Yorkshire Plaza Shopping Center
4358 E. New York Street
Directions: Northwest corner of Route 59 and E. New York Street, across from Fox Valley Mall
Phone: (708) 898–3555
Hours: 10:00 A.M.–9:00 P.M., Monday–Saturday; noon–5:00 P.M., Sunday
Credit Cards: American Express, Discover, Elder-Beerman, MasterCard, Visa
Personal Checks: Yes
Handicapped Accessible: Partial

Food: Available in nearby shopping center or mall
Bus Tours: Yes

Lands' End Outlet Store
Yorkshire Plaza
4320 New York Street

Directions: Across from Fox Valley Mall; I–88 to Route 59 exit, then to Aurora Avenue (New York Street)
Phone: (708) 851–2990
Hours: Call for current schedule.
Credit Cards: American Express, MasterCard, Visa
Personal Checks: Yes, with proper identification
Handicapped Accessible: Yes
Food: Available in shopping center vicinity

CARBONDALE

The Ultimate Outlet
634 E. Walnut

Directions: Off Highway 13, 6 blocks east of the railroad tracks on Walnut Street
Phone: (618) 529–2585
Hours: 10:00 A.M.–6:00 P.M., Monday–Saturday; 1:00 P.M.–5:00 P.M., Sunday
Additional Savings: Sales at the end of each season
Credit Cards: Most major credit cards accepted.
Personal Checks: Yes, with proper identification
Handicapped Accessible: Yes
Food: Available on the block
Bus Tours: Yes
Notes or Attractions: Carbondale in Shawnee National Forest, with lakes, fishing, and outdoor activities

CHICAGO

Adams Factory Shoe Outlet
3655–59 W. Irving Park Road

Directions: Take Route 19/Irving Park Road exit off I–94 and go 1½ miles east.
Phone: (312) 539–4120
Hours: 9:00 A.M.–6:00 P.M., Monday–Saturday; 10:00 A.M.–4:30 P.M., Sunday
Credit Cards: Discover, MasterCard, Visa
Personal Checks: Yes, with proper identification
Handicapped Accessible: Call ahead for assistance; park in back parking lot and store will open back door to let you in.
Food: On the block
Bus Tours: Yes

Burlington Coat Factory Warehouse
two locations:
Harlen and Foster Avenues, 2 blocks south of Kennedy Expressway; (312) 763–6006
81st Street and South Cicero, 2 blocks south of the Ford City Shopping Center; (312) 767–7790

Hours: 10:00 A.M.–9:00 P.M., Monday–Saturday; 11:00 A.M.–6:00 P.M., Sunday.
Credit Cards: MasterCard, Visa
Personal Checks: Yes, with proper identification
Handicapped Accessible: Yes, with designated handicapped parking
Food: Available within a 5-block radius
Bus Tours: Yes

Crate and Barrel Outlet Store
800 W. North Avenue

Directions: Call ahead.

Phone: (312) 787–4775
Hours: 10:00 A.M.–7:00 P.M., Monday–Saturday; 11:00 A.M.–5:00 P.M., Sunday
Additional Savings: Annual end-of-summer sale
Credit Cards: American Express, MasterCard, Visa
Personal Checks: Yes
Handicapped Accessible: Yes, with ramp into store.
Food: Av[illegible]
Bus Tours: Yes

Crawford's Linen Outlet
2523 W. Devon Avenue

Directions: Two blocks west of Western Avenue on Devon
Phone: (312) 338–2500 ext. 234
Hours: 10:00 A.M.–8:00 P.M., Monday and Thursday; 10:00 A.M.–5:30 P.M., Wednesday and Friday; 9:00 A.M.–5:30 P.M., Tuesday; 9:30 A.M.–5:30 P.M., Saturday; 11:00 A.M.–4:00 P.M., Sunday
Additional Savings: July and January dollar days
Credit Cards: Discover, MasterCard, Visa, Crawford charge card
Personal Checks: Yes, with proper identification
Handicapped Accessible: Yes
Food: Six restaurants within walking distance on Devon Avenue
Bus Tours: Yes
Notes or Attractions: Ten percent senior-citizen discount on Tuesday. Validate for two hours' free parking in city lot in rear of store.

Designer's Outlet
6965 N. Clark Street

Directions: Take I–94, exiting at Toughy Avenue; go east to Clark Street; at Clark, turn south.
Phone: (312) 973–4600
Hours: 10:00 A.M.–7:00 P.M., Monday, Tuesday, Thursday, and Friday; 9:00 A.M.–7:00 P.M., Wednesday and Saturday
Additional Savings: Seasonal sales April/May and September/October

Credit Cards: Discover, MasterCard, Visa
Personal Checks: Yes, with driver's license or state picture identification plus home telephone number.
Handicapped Accessible: Yes
Food: Restaurants and fast food available within 1 block
Bus Tours: Yes; call ahead for an appointment.
Notes or Attractions: Outlet serves as cutting contractor for manufacturers and is like a mini factory tour.

El-Bee Shoe Outlet
Dunning Square Shopping Center
6500 Irving Park Road

Directions: Corner of Narragansett and Irving Park Road
Phone: (312) 282–7995
Hours: 10:00 A.M.–9:00 P.M., Monday–Saturday; noon–5:00 P.M., Sunday
Credit Cards: American Express, Discover, Elder-Beerman, MasterCard, Visa
Personal Checks: Yes
Handicapped Accessible: Yes; shopping center parking lot has designated handicapped parking
Food: Available in nearby shopping center or mall
Bus Tours: Yes

Gabel's Men's Wear
5719 N. Central Avenue

Directions: Take Kennedy Expressway (I–90) to Nagle Street exit; turn north (left), proceed to first light (Bryn Mawr Avenue), and make a right onto Central; approximately 2 blocks north on Central.
Phone: (312) 775–3171
Hours: 10:00 A.M.–6:00 P.M., Monday, Wednesday–Friday; 9:00 A.M.–5:00 P.M., Saturday; 10:00 A.M.–4:00 P.M., Sunday
Credit Cards: Discover, MasterCard, Visa
Personal Checks: Yes, with proper identification

Handicapped Accessible: Yes
Food: Restaurants and fast food available within 1 block
Bus Tours: Yes

Jefferson Industries Outlet Store
2100 S. Marshall Boulevard

Directions: Call ahead.
Phone: (312) 277–6100
Hours: 9:00 A.M.–4:00 P.M., Monday–Saturday
Credit Cards: Discover, MasterCard, Visa
Personal Checks: Checks that are covered by Telecheck
Handicapped Accessible: Yes, if accompanied by another person; 6 wide stairs in front of building
Food: Available 2 blocks away
Bus Tours: Yes

Karoll's Outlet Stores
two locations:
1400 S. Clinton; (312) 226–9859
3201 W. 63rd Street; (312) 476–9581

Directions: Call ahead.
Hours: 9:00 A.M.–5:00 P.M., Monday–Friday
Additional Savings: Extra 20 percent discount in July and February
Credit Cards: American Express, Discover, bank credit cards, Karoll's charge
Personal Checks: Yes, with proper identification
Handicapped Accessible: Yes
Food: Several restaurants and snack eateries 2 blocks away
Bus Tours: Yes

Lands' End Outlet
two locations:
2241 N. Elston (women's store); (312) 276–2232
2317 N. Elston (men's store); (312) 384–4170

Directions: Take Kennedy Expressway to Fullerton Avenue; proceed until Elston Avenue, making a right. Stores are on that block.
Hours: 10:00 A.M.–5:00 P.M., Monday–Saturday; noon–5:00 P.M., Sunday
Credit Cards: American Express, MasterCard, Visa
Personal Checks: Yes, with proper identification
Handicapped Accessible: Yes

The Mattress Factory
2850 W. Irving Park Road

Directions: Take Route 19/Irving Park exit off I–94 and go 1½ miles east.
Phone: (312) 478–1239
Hours: 9:00 A.M.–5:00 P.M., Monday–Saturday
Credit Cards: Discover, MasterCard, Visa
Personal Checks: Yes, with a driver's license, state identification card, or major credit card, plus name imprinted on checks
Handicapped Accessible: Yes

Meystel/Rayco Outlet Store
1243 S. Wabash Avenue

Directions: Call ahead.
Phone: (312) 922–5930
Hours: 9:00 A.M.–6:00 P.M., Monday–Friday; 10:00 A.M.–5:00 P.M., Sunday
Credit Cards: All major cards
Personal Checks: Yes, with driver's license
Handicapped Accessible: Yes
Food: Around the corner
Bus Tours: Yes

Smoler Brothers Outlet
2300 W. Wabansia Avenue

Directions: Call ahead.
Phone: (312) 384–1200
Hours: 9:00 A.M.–4:00 P.M., Monday–Wednesday and Friday; 9:00 A.M.–9:00 P.M., Thursday; 9:00 A.M.–3:00 P.M., Saturday
Additional Savings: Before-Easter sales
Credit Cards: No
Personal Checks: Yes, with proper identification
Handicapped Accessible: No
Food: In the vicinity
Bus Tours: Yes

CICERO

Simandl Coats
2506 S. Laramie Avenue

Directions: Five miles south of Eisenhower Expressway (Route 290) on the 5200 block west of Laramie Avenue
Phone: (708) 863–2718
Hours: 10:00 A.M.–4:00 P.M., Monday–Friday; 10:00 A.M.–2:00 P.M., Saturday
Credit Cards: MasterCard, Visa
Personal Checks: Yes, with proper identification
Handicapped Accessible: No
Food: Restaurants in the area
Bus Tours: No

DECATUR

District Factory Outlet
125 E. North Street

Directions: Half block east of Route 51 South and 1 block south of Route 36
Phone: (217) 422–6503
Hours: 10:00 A.M.–6:00 P.M., Monday–Friday; 10:00 A.M.–5:00 P.M., Saturday; noon–5:00 P.M., Sundays October through May
Credit Cards: MasterCard, Visa
Personal Checks: Yes, with driver's license
Handicapped Accessible: Yes
Food: All around downtown area
Bus Tours: No

DOWNERS GROVE

El-Bee Shoe Outlet
Grove Shopping Center
1400 75th Street

Directions: Northwest corner of Lemont Road and 75th Street
Phone: (708) 810–0322
Hours: 10:00 A.M.–9:00 P.M., Monday–Saturday; noon–5:00 P.M., Sunday
Credit Cards: American Express, Discover, Elder-Beerman, MasterCard, Visa
Personal Checks: Yes
Handicapped Accessible: Partial
Food: Available in nearby shopping center or mall
Bus Tours: Yes

Towel Factory Outlet Center
1730 Ogden Avenue

Directions: Call ahead.
Phone: (708) 852–3616
Hours: 9:30 A.M.–9:00 P.M., Monday and Thursday; 9:30 A.M.–6:00 P.M., Tuesday, Wednesday, and Friday; 9:30 A.M.–5:30 P.M., Saturday; 11:00 A.M.–5:00 P.M., Sunday
Additional Savings: Month-long sale of select items
Credit Cards: Most major cards are accepted with a minimum purchase of $20.
Personal Checks: Yes, with proper identification
Handicapped Accessible: Yes
Food: Available in the vicinity
Bus Tours: Yes

EAST DUNDEE

Haegar Pottery Factory Outlet Complex
Van Buren Street

Directions: I–90 to exit 25N at Route 72–Higgins Road. Go west to city of East Dundee. Turn left onto Van Buren Street; outlet complex is in 2 blocks.
Phone: (708) 426–3441
Hours: 8:30 A.M.–5:00 P.M., Monday–Friday; 10:00 A.M.–5:00 P.M., weekends and holidays
Credit Cards: MasterCard, Visa
Personal Checks: Yes, with proper identification
Handicapped Accessible: Yes
Food: Within several blocks
Bus Tours: Yes
Notes or Attractions: Free factory tours arranged by calling (708) 426–3441

Milk Pail Village Factory Outlet Stores
Route 25

Directions: In Fox River Valley, Route 25 north off I–90
Phone: (708) 742–5043
Hours: 10:00 A.M.–8:00 P.M., Tuesday–Saturday; 10:00 A.M.–6:00 P.M., Sunday and Monday
Outlets:
Bass Shoes
Campus Factory Outlet
Capezio Factory Outlet
Houseware Outlet
Leather Manor
Van Heusen Factory Store
Credit Cards: Most stores take major credit cards.
Personal Checks: Yes
Handicapped Accessible: Yes
Food: Restaurant adjacent to mall
Notes or Attractions: Located in beautiful rural setting; wildlife often seen from restaurant.

ELK GROVE

Towel Factory Outlet Center
2404 E. Oakton

Directions: Call ahead.
Phone: (708) 981–1620
Hours: 9:30 A.M.–8:00 P.M., Monday and Thursday; 9:30 A.M.–6:00 P.M., Tuesday, Wednesday, and Friday; 9:30 A.M.–5:00 P.M., Saturday; 11:00 A.M.–5:00 P.M., Sunday
Additional Savings: Month-long sale of select items
Credit Cards: Most major cards are accepted, with a minimum purchase of $20.
Personal Checks: Yes, with proper identification

Handicapped Accessible: Yes
Food: Available in the vicinity
Bus Tours: Yes

EVANSTON

Lands' End Not Quite Perfect Store
816½ Church Street

Directions: Near the intersection of Church and Benson
Phone: (312) 328–3009
Hours: Call for current schedule.
Credit Cards: American Express, MasterCard, Visa
Personal Checks: Yes, with proper identification
Handicapped Accessible: Yes
Food: Fast food within walking distance

FOREST PARK

Karoll's Outlet Stores
Forest Park Mall
7600 W. Roosevelt Road

Directions: Call ahead.
Phone: (708) 771–9020
Hours: 10:00 A.M.–9:00 P.M., Monday–Friday; 10:00 A.M.–6:00 P.M., Saturday; noon–5:00 P.M., Sunday
Additional Savings: Extra 20 percent off in July and February
Credit Cards: American Express, Discover, bank cards, Karoll's charge
Personal Checks: Yes, with identification
Handicapped Accessible: Yes
Food: Fast food in food court
Bus Tours: Yes

FRANKLIN PARK

Todd's
2727 Mannheim Avenue

Directions: Call ahead.
Phone: (708) 451–0024
Hours: 10:00 A.M.–6:00 P.M., Monday–Friday; 10:00 A.M.–5:00 P.M., Saturday; 11:00 A.M.–5:00 P.M., Sunday
Credit Cards: American Express, Discover, MasterCard, Visa
Personal Checks: Yes, with proper identification
Handicapped Accessible: Yes
Food: Fast food within walking distance

GURNEE

Gurnee Mills
Route 132 (Grand Avenue)

Directions: Take 1–94 West (heading north) and exit west at Route 132 (Grand Avenue), just beyond Great America theme park.
Phone: (800) YES–SHOP or (708) 263–7500 in Illinois
Hours: 10:00 A.M.–9:00 P.M., Monday–Saturday; 11:00 A.M.–6 P.M., Sunday
Outlets:
American Tourister
Banister Shoes
Book Warehouse
Brass Factory Outlet
Bugle Boy
Capezio
Casual Male Big and Tall
Dickens Books
Dress Barn

Etienne Aigner
Famous Footware
Finish Line
Florsheim Shoe
Kids Mart Clearance
No Nonsense & More
Paper Factory
Prestige Fragrance
Publishers Outlet
S & K Famous Brands
Sears Outlet
Specials by Levi
Tool Warehouse
Top of the Line Cosmetics
Toy Liquidators
Van Heusen
Waccamaw Pottery
Wemco
Westport

Credit Cards: Most major cards

Personal Checks: Yes (for most merchants) with proper identification

Handicapped Accessible: Yes; wheelchairs available at shopper information booths

Food: Two food courts with nearly twenty snack shops and fast-food and casual restaurants

Notes or Attractions: Strollers available at shopper information booths. Mall near Great America theme park.

> At press time Gurnee Mills had just opened, and much of its space had yet to be leased. Please call the mall's main numbers for information on the dozens of additional outlets that by now are welcoming customers. —Ed.

HANOVER

Whistling Wings
113 Washington Street

Directions: On U.S. Highway 34
Phone: (815) 591–3512
Hours: 9:00 A.M.–5:00 P.M., Monday–Friday; 9:00 A.M.–noon, Saturday
Credit Cards: No
Personal Checks: Yes, with proper identification
Handicapped Accessible: Yes
Food: Within a block
Bus Tours: Yes
Notes or Attractions: Sixteen miles from Galena near Mississippi Palisades State Park, downhill skiing, and the Mississippi River

HOMETOWN

Towel Factory Outlet Center
8729 S. Cicero

Directions: Call ahead.
Phone: (708) 424–4866
Hours: 10:00 A.M.–9:00 P.M., Monday–Friday; 9:30 A.M.–5:00 P.M., Saturday; 11:00 A.M.–5:00 P.M., Sunday
Additional Savings: Month-long sale of select items
Credit Cards: Most major cards accepted, with a minimum purchase of $20.
Personal Checks: Yes, with proper identification
Handicapped Accessible: Yes
Food: Available in the vicinity
Bus Tours: Yes

HOMEWOOD

Karoll's Outlet Stores
Washington Square Mall
17835 S. Halsted Street

Directions: Call ahead.
Phone: (708) 799–4509
Hours: 10:00 A.M.–9:00 P.M., Monday–Friday; 10:00 A.M.–6:00 P.M., Saturday; noon–5:00 P.M., Sunday
Additional Savings: Extra 20 percent off in July and February
Credit Cards: American Express, Discover, bank cards, Karoll's charge
Personal Checks: Yes, with proper identification
Handicapped Accessible: Yes
Food: In mall
Bus Tours: Yes

KANKAKEE

Graham Industries Home Furnishings Factory Outlet
200 N. Schuyler

Directions: Take I–57 to exit 312 west (Court Street). Continue on Court till Schuyler Avenue; turn right. Outlet is at first light.
Phone: (815) 932–0008
Hours: 10:00 A.M.–5:00 P.M., Monday–Friday; 9:00 A.M.–3:00 P.M., Saturday
Credit Cards: MasterCard, Visa
Personal Checks: Yes, with photo identification
Handicapped Accessible: Yes
Food: Restaurants and fast food within 1½ miles
Bus Tours: Yes, with advance notice

LIBERTYVILLE

Burlington Coat Factory Warehouse
920 Milwaukee Avenue

Directions: Two miles north of Hawthorne Shopping Center
Phone: (708) 680–8150 or (708) 367–0616, shoe department
Hours: 10:00 A.M.–9:00 P.M., Monday–Friday; 10:00 A.M.–6:00 P.M., Saturday; 11:00 A.M.–5:00 P.M., Sunday
Credit Cards: MasterCard, Visa
Personal Checks: Yes, with proper identification
Handicapped Accessible: Yes
Food: In nearby shopping district and Hawthorne Shopping Center
Bus Tours: Yes

LOMBARD

Lands' End Combo Store
Yorktown Convenience Center
Butterfield and Highland Roads

Directions: Exit I–88 at Highland Road
Phone: (708) 953–8855
Hours: Call for current schedule.
Credit Cards: American Express, MasterCard, Visa
Personal Checks: Yes, with two forms of proper identification
Handicapped Accessible: Yes
Food: Available in shopping center vicinity

MACOMB

Haeger Pottery Outlet Store
411 W. Calhoun Street

Directions: Near the intersection of routes 67 and 136
Phone: (309) 833–2171
Hours: 8:30 A.M.–5:00 P.M., Monday–Friday; 10:00 A.M.–5:00 P.M., weekends and holidays
Credit Cards: MasterCard, Visa
Personal Checks: Yes, with two forms of proper identification
Handicapped Accessible: Yes; come in through parking lot
Food: Fast food behind outlet; other fast food and restaurants about 6 blocks away
Bus Tours: Yes
Notes or Attractions: Call to arrange a free factory tour. Macomb is near Argyle Lake State Park and 50 miles from Nauvoo, Illinois, site of one of the largest early Mormon settlements.

MELROSE PARK

Towel Factory Outlet Center
1511 W. North Avenue

Directions: Call ahead.
Phone: (708) 343–6666
Hours: 10:00 A.M.–9:00 P.M., Monday–Friday; 9:30 A.M.–5:00 P.M., Saturday; 11:00 A.M.–5:00 P.M., Sunday
Credit Cards: Most major credit cards are accepted, with a minimum purchase of $20.
Personal Checks: Yes, with proper identification
Handicapped Accessible: Yes
Food: Available in the vicinity
Bus Tours: Yes

MORTON GROVE

Lands' End Outlet Store
6131 W. Dempster

Directions: Dempster between Edens Expressway and Waukegan Road; I–94 to Dempster exit
Phone: (708) 470–0320
Hours: Call for current schedule.
Credit Cards: American Express, MasterCard, Visa
Personal Checks: Yes, with two forms of proper identification
Handicapped Accessible: Yes
Food: Available in shopping center vicinity

NILES

Crawford's Linen Outlet
8257 Golf Road

Directions: In Four Flaggs Shopping Center at the intersection of Golf and Milwaukee
Phone: (708) 965–2270
Hours: 10:00 A.M.–8:00 P.M., Monday–Friday; 9:30 A.M.–5:30 P.M., Saturday; noon–5:00 P.M., Sunday
Additional Savings: Dollar-days sales in January and July
Credit Cards: Discover, MasterCard, Visa, Crawford charge
Personal Checks: Yes, with proper identification
Handicapped Accessible: Yes
Food: Fast food at front of parking lot, food court across the street in Golf Mill Center
Bus Tours: Yes
Notes or Attractions: Ten percent senior-citizen discounts on all merchandise Tuesdays

Towel Factory Outlet Center
7313 N. Harlem Avenue

Directions: Call ahead.
Phone: (312) 792–1700
Hours: 9:30 A.M.–9:00 P.M., Monday and Thursday; 9:30 A.M.–5:00 P.M., Tuesday, Wednesday, Friday, and Saturday; 11:00 A.M.–5:00 P.M., Sunday
Additional Savings: Month-long sales of select items
Credit Cards: Most major cards, with minimum purchase of $20.
Personal Checks: Yes, with proper identification
Handicapped Accessible: Yes
Food: Available in the vicinity
Bus Tours: Yes

ORLAND PARK

Lands' End Outlet
Lake View Plaza
159th and LaGrange Road

Directions: I–80 to 96th Avenue exit; continue 1 block where 96th Avenue turns into LaGrange Road at the intersection of 159th.
Phone: (708) 403–2020
Hours: 10:00 A.M.–9:00 P.M., Monday–Friday; 10:00 A.M.–6:00 P.M., Saturday; 11:00 A.M.–5:00 P.M., Sunday
Credit Cards: American Express, MasterCard, Visa
Personal Checks: Yes, with two forms of proper identification
Handicapped Accessible: Yes
Food: Near shopping plaza

ROCKFORD

Forest Plaza
State and Mulford Roads

Directions: I–90 to Business Route 20 (State Street) exit west; plaza is approximately 1½ miles away.
Phone: Outdoor plaza—no on-site phone
Hours: 10:00 A.M.–9:00 P.M., Monday–Friday; 10:00 A.M.–5:30 P.M., Saturday; noon–5:00 P.M., Sunday
Outlets:
Bass Shoe Outlet
El-Bee Shoe Outlet
Factory Card Outlet
Famous Footwear
Kids Mart
Shapes Active Outlet
Van Heusen Factory Outlet
Credit Cards: Most stores accept most major credit cards.
Personal Checks: Most stores will accept checks with two forms of proper identification.
Handicapped Accessible: Yes
Food: Restaurants and fast-food establishments are located near shopping center.
Bus Tours: Yes
Notes or Attractions: Fourteen museums are located in Rockford.

ST. CHARLES

El-Bee Shoe Outlet
St. Charles Mall
2067 Prairie Street

Directions: At intersection of Route 38 and Randall Road
Phone: (708) 584–5560
Hours: 10:00 A.M.–9:00 P.M., Monday–Saturday; noon–5:00 P.M., Sunday

Credit Cards: American Express, Discover, Elder-Beerman, MasterCard, Visa
Personal Checks: Yes
Handicapped Accessible: Partial
Food: Available in and around mall
Bus Tours: Yes

The Piano Factory Outlet Mall
410 S. First Street

Directions: Three blocks south of Route 64 on First Street
Phone: (708) 584–2099
Hours: 10:00 A.M.–9:00 P.M., Monday–Friday; 10:00 A.M.–6:00 P.M., Saturday; 11:00 A.M.–5:00 P.M., Sunday
Outlets:
Aileen Factory Store
American Tourister Factory Outlet
Aunt Mary's Yarns
Banister Shoes
Bass Shoe Factory Outlet
Book Warehouse
Campus Factory Store
Cape Isle Knitters
Carter's Childrenswear
Chicago Records
Claires Clearance
Corning Factory Store
danray Lingerie
Factory Card Outlet
Gitano Factory Store
harvé benard
The Houseware Outlet Store
Jonathan Logan
Just Pants
Kitchen Collection
Leather Manor
L'eggs/Hanes/Bali
Manhattan Factory Outlet

New England Classics
Pfaltzgraff Collector's Center
Prevue Fashions
Sweat Graphics
Temptations Jewelry
Top of the Line Cosmetics
Van Heusen Factory Store
What A Deal
Credit Cards: Most stores accept most major credit cards.
Personal Checks: Most stores accept checks with two forms of proper identification.
Handicapped Accessible: Yes
Food: Bakery/cafe within the mall
Bus Tours: Yes
Notes or Attractions: On the scenic bank of the Fox River, mall is housed in a renovated piano factory.

SCHAUMBURG

Lands' End Outlet
The Annex
251 W. Golf Road

Directions: Near the intersection of Route 58 (Golf Road) and Route 72 (Higgins Road)
Phone: (708) 884–1900
Hours: 10:00 A.M.–9:00 P.M., Monday–Friday; 10:00 A.M.–6:00 P.M., Saturday; 11:00 A.M.–5:00 P.M., Sunday
Credit Cards: American Express, MasterCard, Visa
Personal Checks: Yes, with two forms of proper identification
Handicapped Accessible: Yes
Food: Near shopping center

Meadows Town Mall
Golf and Algonquin Roads

Directions: Take I–90 to Golf Road exit; continue to Algonquin Road.
Phone: (708) 952–1030
Hours: 10:00 A.M.–9:00 P.M., Monday–Friday; 10:00 A.M.–6:00 P.M., Saturday; 11:00 A.M.–5:00 P.M., Sunday
Outlets:
Bag and Baggage
Crown Jewels
Dress Barn
Dress Barn Woman
Factory Card Outlet
Famous Footwear
F & M Distributors
Hit or Miss
Kids Mart
Linens 'n Things
Loomcraft Home Decorating Fabrics
Waccamaw Pottery
Credit Cards: Most merchants accept major credit cards.
Personal Checks: Most will accept checks with a driver's license and major credit card.
Handicapped Accessible: Yes
Food: Restaurants and fast food within the mall

SKOKIE

The Wear House
7700 Gross Point Road

Directions: Between Oakton and Howard, west of Edens Highway
Phone: (708) 966–1282
Hours: 10:00 A.M.–4:30 P.M., Monday–Friday; 10:00 A.M.–3:00 P.M., Saturday, Labor Day to Memorial Day; 9:00 A.M.–noon, Saturday, summer

Additional Savings: Three seasonal sales yearly
Credit Cards: Cash only
Personal Checks: Cash only
Handicapped Accessible: Yes
Food: None nearby
Bus Tours: Yes

SOUTH CHICAGO HEIGHTS

Oops We Goofed
18 East Sauk Trail

Directions: Three miles west of I–394 on Sauk Trail
Phone: (708) 754–5250
Hours: 10:00 A.M.–5:00 P.M., Monday–Saturday
Additional Savings: Spring clearance usually in May
Credit Cards: Discover, MasterCard, Visa
Personal Checks: Yes, with proper identification
Handicapped Accessible: Yes
Food: Eight restaurants within ½ mile
Bus Tours: Yes

VILLA PARK

Burlington Coat Factory Warehouse
Villa Oaks Shopping Center

Directions: Ardmore and Roosevelt roads
Phone: (708) 832–4500
Hours: 10:00 A.M.–9:00 P.M., Monday–Friday; 10:00 A.M.–6:00 P.M., Saturday; 11:00 A.M.–5:00 P.M., Sunday
Credit Cards: MasterCard, Visa

Personal Checks: Yes, with proper identification
Handicapped Accessible: Yes
Food: In the immediate vicinity near the shopping center and mall

J. C. Penney Catalog Outlet
250 W. North Avenue

Directions: In North Park Mall at the corner of North Avenue (Route 64) and Addision Road
Phone: (708) 279–1700
Hours: 9:30 A.M.–9:00 P.M., Monday–Friday; 9:30 A.M.–6:00 P.M., Saturday; 10:00 A.M.–6:00 P.M., Sunday
Credit Cards: American Express, J. C. Penney, MasterCard, Visa
Personal Checks: Yes, with proper identification
Handicapped Accessible: Yes
Food: Available within the mall
Bus Tours: Yes

Karoll's Outlet Stores
North Park Mall
270 W. North Avenue

Directions: Call ahead.
Phone: (708) 833–4989
Hours: 10:00 A.M.–9:00 P.M., Monday–Friday; 10:00 A.M.–6:00 P.M., Saturday; 11:00 A.M.–5:00 P.M., Sunday
Credit Cards: American Express, Discover, bank cards, Karoll's charge
Personal Checks: Yes, with proper identification
Handicapped Accessible: Yes
Food: In and near the mall

WARREN

Warren Cheese Plant
415 Jefferson Street

Directions: North of U.S. 20, a few blocks west of Highway 78
Phone: (815) 745–2627
Hours: 8:00 A.M.–4:00 P.M., Monday–Friday; 8:00 A.M.–noon, Saturday
Credit Cards: No
Personal Checks: Yes, with proper identification
Handicapped Accessible: Yes
Food: Cafes on Main Street, 4 blocks away
Bus Tours: Yes
Notes or Attractions: Apple River Canyon State Park nearby; paddle-wheeler river cruises are out of historic Galena, which is 30 miles away.

WEST FRANKFORT

VF Factory Outlet Mall
1000 Factory Outlet Drive

Directions: I–57 to exit 65, making a left across the road at West Frankfort
Phone: (618) 937–3536
Hours: 9:00 A.M.–7:00 P.M., Monday–Thursday; 9:00 A.M.–9:00 P.M., Friday and Saturday; noon–5:00 P.M., Sunday
Outlets:
Banister Shoe
Bass Shoe Outlet
Bon Worth
The Paper Factory
Prestige Fragrance & Cosmetics

Van Heusen Factory Store
VF Factory Outlet
Wallet Works
Credit Cards: MasterCard, Visa; some stores take additional cards
Personal Checks: Yes, with proper identification
Handicapped Accessible: Yes
Food: Sandwiches, salads, and snacks available in the mall
Bus Tours: Yes

Remember that outlets accepting personal checks require at least two forms of proper identification, usually a driver's license and a major credit card.

INDIANA

Numbers to the left of entries in this legend correspond to the numbers on the accompanying map. The number to the right of each city's or town's name is the page number on which that municipality's outlets first appear.

INDIANA

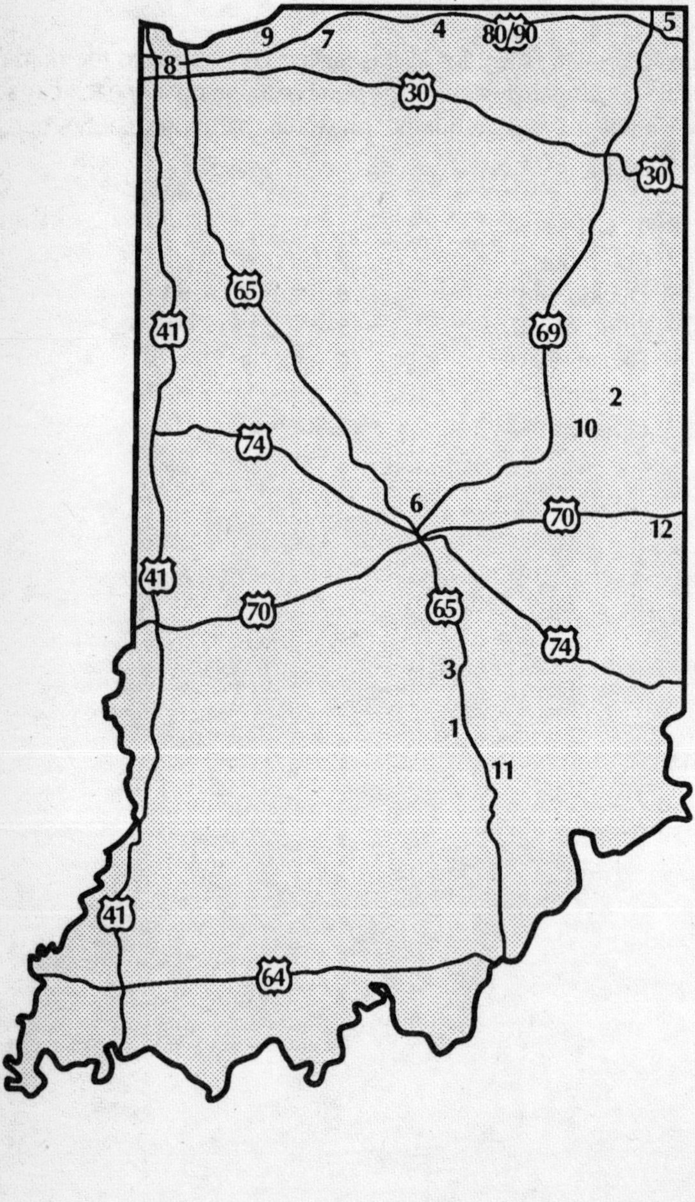

COLUMBUS

Cosco Factory Outlet Store
2525 State Street

Directions: I–65 to Highway 7 South, 4 miles
Phone: (812) 372–0141
Hours: January through September 11:30 A.M.–5:00 P.M., Monday–Friday; October through December 10:00 A.M.–6:00 P.M., Monday–Friday; 10:00 A.M.–2:00 P.M., Saturday
Credit Cards: MasterCard, Visa
Personal Checks: Yes
Handicapped Accessible: Yes
Food: Local restaurants with wide selections of food
Bus Tours: By appointment only

El-Bee Shoe Outlet
Fair Oaks Mall
2292 25th Street

Directions: I–65 to Route 31 South 9 miles, mall on right
Phone: (812) 372–3831
Hours: 10:00 A.M.–9:00 P.M., Monday–Saturday; noon–5:00 P.M., Sunday
Credit Cards: American Express, Discover, Elder-Beerman, MasterCard, Visa
Personal Checks: Yes
Handicapped Accessible: Partial
Food: Available in or near shopping center
Bus Tours: Yes

DUNKIRK

Indiana Glass Outlet
1059 S. Main

Directions: State Road 67N to 167 North. Turn left into outlet store at the factory.
Phone: (317) 768–7889
Hours: 10:00 A.M.–4:00 P.M., Tuesday–Saturday
Additional Savings: Sales during the Dunkirk Glass Festival (last weekend in May through first week in June)
Credit Cards: MasterCard, Visa
Personal Checks: Yes, with driver's license
Handicapped Accessible: Yes
Food: Drive-in across the street
Bus Tours: Yes
Notes or Attractions: Near Dunkirk Glass Museum with 3,000 pieces of glass from eighty-five factories. Museum open from May 1 through November 1.

EDINBURG

Manufacturers Marketplace
11626 N.E. Executive Drive

Directions: On U.S. 31 at the I–65 junction; exit at 76B (Edinburg/Columbus).
Phone: (616) 728–5170
Hours: 10:00 A.M.–9:00 P.M., Monday–Saturday; 11:00 A.M.–7:00 P.M., Sunday
Outlets:
Aileen
Ambassador Crystal
American Tourister
Aunt Mary's Yarn

Banister Shoes
Barbizon
Bass Shoe
Big and Better
Bon Worth
Book Warehouse
Cape Isle Knitters
Country Source
Famous Designer Outlet
Farah Factory Store
Fashion Flair (Izod)
Fieldcrest Cannon
Fragrance World
Gitano
Hanes Activewear
Ideas
Just My Size
KidsPort USA
Kitchen Collection
Knits by K.T.
Leather Loft
L'eggs/Hanes/Bali
Little Red Shoe House
Mackintosh of New England
Made In Italy
Maidenform
Manhattan
Nickels Company Store
Old Mill
The Paper Factory
Ribbon Outlet
Scents and Soaps
Socks Galore
Specials by Levi Strauss & Co.
Stone Mountain Handbags
Swank
Tiffany Lamp Factory Outlet
Tool Warehouse
Toy Liquidators

Van Heusen
Wallet Works
Welcome Home
WestPort, Ltd.
Windsor Shirt
Wooden Bench

Credit Cards: Most merchants accept major credit cards.
Personal Checks: Most merchants accept checks with two forms of proper identification
Handicapped Accessible: One-level shopping
Food: Food court with a variety of hot foods and snacks. Free indoor playland for the kids is located in food court.
Bus Tours: Yes, discount coupons and shopping bags for tour participants
Notes or Attractions: Near Brown County State Park

ELKHART

Value Center
1333 S. Nappanee Street

Directions: One mile south of Indiana Highway 20 and ½ mile north of Indiana Highway 33 on Nappanee Street (Highway 19)
Phone: (219) 293–0111; fax: (219) 293–2333
Hours: 10:00 A.M.–9:00 P.M., Monday–Saturday
Additional Savings: Seasonal sales during summer and after Christmas; large savings on slightly damaged, less current goods in bargain basement
Credit Cards: MasterCard, Visa
Personal Checks: Local only (within 50 miles)
Handicapped Accessible: Yes
Food: In the neighborhood
Bus Tours: Yes
Notes or Attractions: Near Indiana Amish country. Elkhart is the RV

capital of the country, with many manufacturers and van conversion companies located in town.

FREMONT

Valley Outlet Center
Intersection of Indiana toll road 80-90 and I–69

Directions: 45 miles north of Fort Wayne, at the intersection of I–80/90 and I–69
Phone: (219) 833–1684
Hours: 10:00 A.M.–9:00 P.M., Monday–Saturday; 11:00 A.M.–6:00 P.M., Sunday
Outlets:
Aileen
Aunt Mary's Yarns
Banister Shoes
Cape Craftsmen
Clothesworks
Corning Glass
Fashion Flair (Izod)
G. H. Bass
Gitano
Hanes Activewear
Jaymar
Just My Size (Hanes)
KidsPort USA
Kitchen Collection
Leather Manor
L'eggs/Hanes/Bali
Little Red Shoe House
Manhattan
Old Mill
Salem China

Socks Galore
Top of the Line Cosmetics
totes
Toy Liquidators
Van Heusen
Warnaco

Credit Cards: Most merchants accept major credit cards.
Personal Checks: Most merchants accept checks with two forms of proper identification.
Handicapped Accessible: One-level shopping
Food: Pizza shop on premises
Bus Tours: Yes
Notes or Attractions: Bank on premises. Mall is near Pokagon State Park on the shores of Lake James, close to the Michigan border.

INDIANAPOLIS

Eastgate Consumer Mall
7150 E. Washington Street

Directions: Take the West Washington Street exit off I–465 ½ mile. Center is on the right.
Phone: (317) 352–0951
Hours: 10:00 A.M.–9:00 P.M., Monday–Saturday; noon–5:00 P.M., Sunday
Additional Savings: Sidewalk clearance sales in second week of January and second week of July
Outlets:
Blume Jewelers
Burlington Coat Factory
The Children's Outlet
Creations By Elaine
Dr. Tavel's Premium Optical
El-Bee Shoe Outlet

Famous Footwear
F & M Distributors
The Finish Line
Hit or Miss
Jewelies
Linens 'n Things
Masters Fashion Center
Old Mill Ladies Factory Outlet
Rosewood Galleries
Sizes Unlimited
Village Clock Shop
Credit Cards: Most stores accept major credit cards.
Personal Checks: Most merchants accept checks with two forms of proper identification.
Handicapped Accessible: Yes, with wheelchair available
Food: Food court in the mall with a variety of snacks and foods
Bus Tours: Yes

El-Bee Shoe Outlet
two locations:
7150 E. Washington Street—Take West Washington Street exit off I–465 ½ mile; center is on the right; (317) 353–2911
Nora Plaza, 1300 E. Eighty-Sixth Street—I–465 to Highway 431 South until Nora-Castleton exit; right from exit 1½ miles; center on right; (317) 848–4029

Hours: 10:00 A.M.–9:00 P.M., Monday–Saturday; noon–5:00 P.M., Sunday
Credit Cards: American Express, Discover, Elder-Beerman, MasterCard, Visa
Personal Checks: Yes
Handicapped Accessible: Partial
Food: Available in or near shopping center
Bus Tours: Yes

LAPORTE

Kingsley Factory Furniture Outlet Store
102 Park Street

Directions: Call ahead.
Phone: (219) 326–0550
Hours: 10:00 A.M.–4:00 P.M., Friday; 9:00 A.M.–1:00 P.M., Saturday
Credit Cards: Visa
Personal Checks: No
Handicapped Accessible: No
Food: Fast food and restaurants within 1 mile
Bus Tours: Yes
Notes or Attractions: Near Lake Michigan and the Indiana Dunes

MERRILLVILLE

Century Mall
8311 Broadway

Directions: West of I–65 on Highway 30
Phone: (219) 769–3417
Hours: 10:00 A.M.–9:00 P.M., Monday–Saturday; noon–6:00 P.M., Sunday
Outlets:
Burlington Coat Factory Warehouse
Casual Male Big and Tall
Factory Card Outlet
Famous Footwear
The Finish Line
Hit or Miss
Royal Belgian Rug Outlet
Sizes Unlimited
Tiffany Lamp Factory Outlet
Van Heusen Factory Store

Credit Cards: Most stores accept major credit cards.
Personal Checks: Most merchants accept checks with two forms of proper identification.
Handicapped Accessible: shops all on one level
Food: A variety of fast foods, snacks, and restaurants is available within the mall.
Bus Tours: Yes

El-Bee Shoe Outlet
Merrillville Plaza
1876 E. 80th Street

Directions: On U.S. 30 ½ mile east of I–65, across from Southlake Mall
Phone: (219) 756–4001
Hours: 10:00 A.M.–9:00 P.M., Monday–Saturday; noon–5:00 P.M., Sunday
Credit Cards: American Express, Discover, Elder-Beerman, MasterCard, Visa
Personal Checks: Yes
Handicapped Accessible: Partial
Food: Available in or near shopping center
Bus Tours: Yes

MICHIGAN CITY

Burnham Glove Outlet
Wall Street

Directions: Exit onto 421 North from I–94 to Highway 20 at Marquette Mall; go left on Highway 20. At first light (Ohio Street), make a right. Travel to 1600 block until you see a gray sandstone building on left with Burnham sign.

Phone: (219) 874–5205
Hours: 8:00 A.M.–4:00 P.M., weekdays; 9:00 A.M.–noon, Saturday (9:00 A.M.–3:00 P.M., from November 3 to February 23)
Additional Savings: Ten percent off during last two weeks in February
Credit Cards: MasterCard, Visa
Personal Checks: Yes
Handicapped Accessible: Yes
Food: Six blocks away
Bus Tours: Yes
Notes or Attractions: Near Lighthouse Place Factory Outlet Center, Lake Michigan, and Indiana Dunes

Hickey-Freeman
The Works, 711 Wabash Street

Directions: From I–94 or Indiana toll road 80-90, take the Michigan City exit north to 6th Street. Go left on 6th to Lighthouse Place.
Phone: (219) 873–9051
Hours (Central Time): 9:00 A.M.–8:00 P.M., Monday–Saturday; 10:00 A.M.–6:00 P.M., Sunday and holidays
Credit Cards: Most major cards
Personal Checks: Yes, with proper identification
Handicapped Accessible: Yes
Food: At Lighthouse Factory Outlet Mall across the street
Bus Tours: Yes
Notes or Attractions: Lighthouse Place Outlet Center (next listing)

Lighthouse Place Outlet Center
6th and Wabash Streets

Directions: From I–94 or Indiana toll road 80-90, take the Michigan City exit north to 6th Street. Go left on 6th to Lighthouse Place.
Phone: Visitor Information, (219) 879–6506; Business Office, (219) 874–2915
Hours (Central Time): 9:00 A.M.–8:00 P.M., Monday–Saturday; 10:00 A.M.–6:00 P.M., Sunday and holidays

Additional Savings: Sidewalk sale last weekend in August and warehouse sale in January
Outlets:
Aileen Outlet
American Tourister
Anko Also
Anne Klein Outlet
Banister Shoes
Bass Shoe Outlet
Benetton
BG Chicago
Brands Fashion Factory Outlet
Capezio Shoes
Carter's Childrenswear
Corning/Revere Factory Store
Crystal Works
Dansk Factory Outlet
Fanny Farmer Candy Outlet
Fashion Flair/Izod
Fieldcrest Cannon
14 Plus Pizazz
Gitano
Hanes Activewear
harvé benard
Hathaway Factory
I.B. Diffusions
Jaymar Factory Outlet
J.H. Collectibles Factory Outlet
Jindo Furs
Jonathan Logan Factory Outlet
Just Pants Warehouse
Kitchen Collection
Leather Manor
L'eggs/Hanes/Bali
Maidenform Outlet
Manhattan Factory Outlet
Multiples Outlet
Mushrooms
Oneida Silver Factory Outlet

The Paper Factory
Polo/Ralph Lauren
Prestige Fragrance and Cosmetics
The Ribbon Outlet
Royal Doulton
Sassafras
Socks Galore
Ties, Etc.
Toy Liquidators
TrendSetters
Van Heusen Factory Outlet
The Wallet Works
Warnaco
Welcome Home
Credit Cards: Most major cards
Personal Checks: Yes, with proper identification
Handicapped Accessible: Yes
Food: Restaurants and snack shops in center
Bus Tours: Yes, with special discounts for groups
Notes or Attractions: Located close to the beaches of Lake Michigan, parks, a zoo, art galleries, museums, and the Indiana Dunes; an hour's drive from downtown Chicago

MUNCIE

El-Bee Shoe Outlet
Northwest Shopping Center
1605 W. McGalliard Road

Directions: I–69 to Route 332 East for 10 miles; shopping center on right
Phone: (317) 284–2170
Hours: 10:00 A.M.–9:00 P.M., Monday–Saturday; noon–5:00 P.M., Sunday
Credit Cards: American Express, Discover, Elder-Beerman, MasterCard, Visa

Personal Checks: Yes
Handicapped Accessible: Partial
Food: Available in or near shopping center
Bus Tours: Yes

Indiana Glass Outlet
1300 Batavia Avenue

Directions: Twelve miles east of I–69 on State Road 32
Phone: (317) 282–7646
Hours: 10:00 A.M.–6:00 P.M., Wednesday–Saturday; noon–5:00 P.M., Sunday
Credit Cards: MasterCard, Visa
Personal Checks: Yes, with driver's license
Handicapped Accessible: Yes
Food: Fast food and restaurants nearby
Bus Tours: Yes
Notes or Attractions: Near Ball Canning Jar Museum, Ball State University Planetarium and Observatory, Minnetrista Cultural Center, and the Muncie Children's Museum with a replica of Garfield the Cat.

NORTH VERNON

Regal Rugs Factory Outlet
100 S. Madison Avenue

Directions: From the intersection of Highways 3, 7, and 50 in North Vernon, go to first stoplight and make a right. Outlet is ½ block down on the left at the base of the phone tower.
Phone: (812) 346–0234
Hours: 10:00 A.M.–5:00 P.M., Monday–Saturday
Credit Cards: Discover, MasterCard, Visa
Personal Checks: Yes

Handicapped Accessible: Yes
Food: Fast food available 1 mile from store
Bus Tours: Yes
Notes or Attractions: One-half hour from Manufacturers Mall in Edinburgh and from Columbus, known for its unique architecture; forty-five minutes from Nashville, Indiana, Louisville, Kentucky, Cincinnati, Ohio, Indianapolis, Indiana, and Brown County State Park.

RICHMOND

El-Bee Shoe Outlet
Gateway Shopping Center
4633 E. Main

Directions: I–70 to Route 27 South for 1½ miles; shopping center on left
Phone: (317) 966–9533
Hours: 10:00 A.M.–9:00 P.M., Monday–Saturday; noon–5:00 P.M., Sunday
Credit Cards: American Express, Discover, Elder-Beerman, MasterCard, Visa
Personal Checks: Yes
Handicapped Accessible: Partial
Food: Available in or near shopping center
Bus Tours: Yes

London Fog Outlet Store
3801 National Road East

Directions: From I–70, take exit 156A to 40 West. Store is 2 miles farther at Richmond Square Mall.
Phone: (317) 966–1021
Hours: 10:00 A.M.–9:00 P.M., Monday–Saturday; noon–5:00 P.M., Sunday

Credit Cards: MasterCard, Visa
Personal Checks: Yes, with two forms of proper identification
Handicapped Accessible: Yes
Food: Available in the mall
Bus Tours: Yes
Notes or Attractions: Near Nettle Creek Factory Outlet and Fairground Village Mall (scheduled to open in summer 1991).

Nettle Creek Factory Outlet
2200 Peacock Road

Directions: Take I–70 to Route 35 South; turn left on Peacock Road. Outlet is several miles down on right-hand side.
Phone: (317) 962–1555
Hours: 9:00 A.M.–5:30 P.M., Monday–Friday; 9:00 A.M.–5:30 P.M., Saturday; noon–4:00 P.M., Sunday
Credit Cards: MasterCard, Visa
Personal Checks: Yes, with proper identification
Handicapped Accessible: No ramp, two stairs to access main entrance. In some portions of the outlet, aisles are tight for wheelchairs.
Food: On Route 35
Bus Tours: Yes

Can't remember what products a particular outlet offers? Check our "Profiles" section beginning on page one. Many listings also contain information on brand names and range of discounts.

IOWA

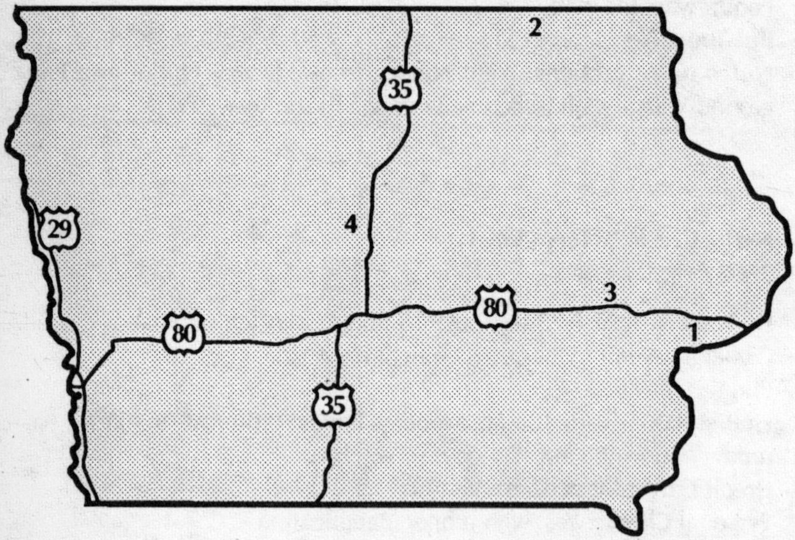

IOWA

Numbers to the left of entries in this legend correspond to the numbers on the accompanying map. The number to the right of each city's or town's name is the page number on which that municipality's outlets first appear.

BETTENDORF

El-Bee Shoe Outlet
Duck Creek Mall
852 Middle Road

Directions: I–74 till Middle Road exit; mall on corner of Middle Road and Kimberly Avenue
Phone: (319) 359–1786
Hours: 10:00 A.M.–9:00 P.M., Monday–Saturday; noon–5:00 P.M., Sunday
Credit Cards: American Express, Discover, Elder-Beerman, MasterCard, Visa
Personal Checks: Yes
Handicapped Accessible: Partial
Food: In mall
Bus Tours: Yes

CHESTER

J & S Liquidators
Highway 63

Directions: On Highway 63 in downtown Chester, 1 mile from the Minnesota border
Phone: (319) 565–4065
Hours: 9:00 A.M.–7:30 P.M., Monday–Thursday; 9:00 A.M.–9:00 P.M., Friday and Saturday; 11:00 A.M.–6:00 P.M., Sunday
Credit Cards: MasterCard, Visa
Personal Checks: Yes
Handicapped Accessible: Yes
Food: Available within the store with restaurants across the street
Bus Tours: Yes
Notes or Attractions: The historic brick building, on the scenic Upper

Iowa River, houses J & S Liquidators and a number of antique and craft shops.

IOWA CITY

Lands' End Outlet Store
10 S. Clinton Street

Directions: From I–80, take the Dubuque Street exit south, then take a right onto Iowa Avenue and a left onto Clinton. Outlet is on left.
Phone: (319) 338–2660
Hours: 10:00 A.M.–8:00 P.M., Monday and Thursday; 10:00 A.M.–6:00 P.M., Tuesday, Wednesday, Friday, and Saturday; noon–5:00 P.M., Sunday
Credit Cards: American Express, MasterCard, Visa
Personal Checks: Yes, with driver's license and major credit card
Handicapped Accessible: First floor only
Food: Available on the same block
Bus Tours: Yes
Notes or Attractions: Near Amana colonies

STORY CITY

VF Factory Outlet Complex
324 Factory Outlet Drive

Directions: I–35 to Route 115 at Broad Street, one hour north of Des Moines
Phone: (515) 733–5242
Hours: 9:00 A.M.–7:00 P.M., Monday–Thursday; 9:00 A.M.–9:00 P.M., Friday and Saturday; noon–6:00 P.M., Sunday

Outlets:
Banister Shoes
Bass Shoe Outlet
Bon Worth
Fieldcrest Cannon
Prestige Fragrance & Cosmetics, Inc.
Van Heusen Factory Store
VF Factory Outlet
The Wallet Works
Credit Cards: MasterCard, Visa
Personal Checks: Yes, with proper identification
Handicapped Accessible: Yes
Bus Tours: Yes

Remember that outlets accepting personal checks require at least two forms of proper identification, usually a driver's license and a major credit card.

MICHIGAN

Numbers to the left of entries in this legend correspond to the numbers on the accompanying map. The number to the right of each city's or town's name is the page number on which that municipality's outlets first appear.

MICHIGAN

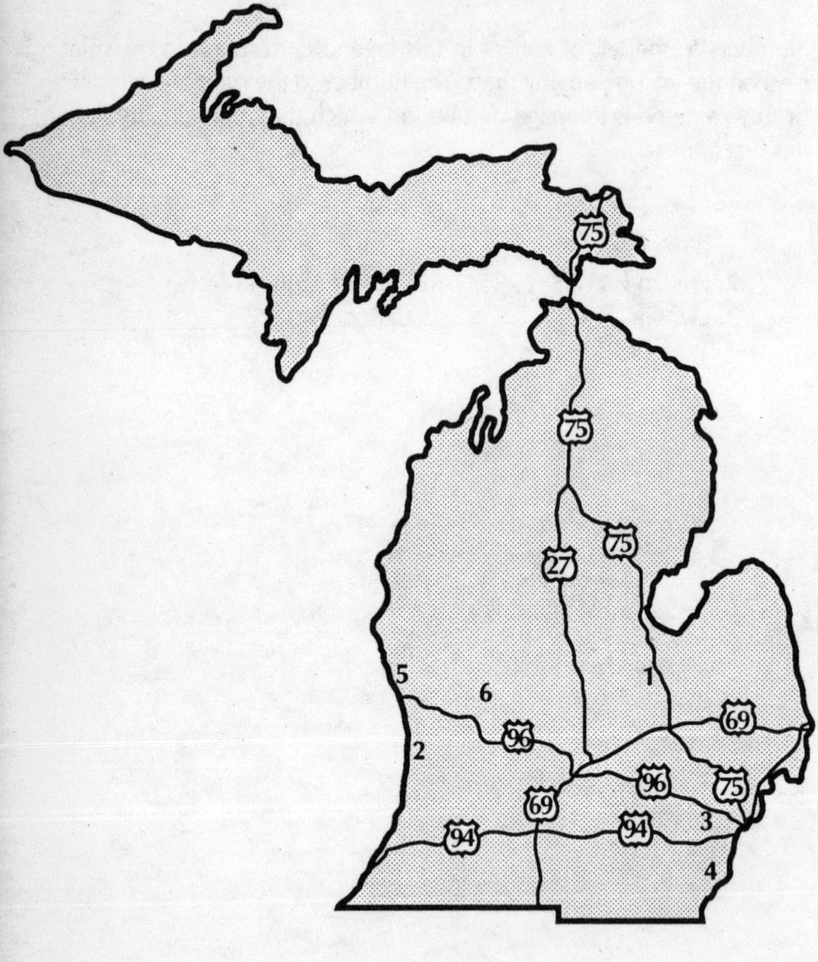

BIRCH RUN

Manufacturers Marketplace
Beyer Road and I–75

Directions: Exit 136 Birch Run/Frankenmuth off I–75
Phone: (517) 624-9348
Hours: 10:00 A.M.–9:00 P.M., Monday–Saturday; 11:00 A.M.–7:00 P.M., Sunday
Outlets:
Aileen
American Tourister
Aunt Mary's Yarns
Banister Shoes
Barbizon Lingerie
Bass Shoes
Becca
Book Warehouse
Cape Isle Knitters
Captree
Carter's Childrenswear
Chicago Records
Cluett
Corning/Revere Factory Store
Dress Barn
Fanny Farmer
Farah Factory Store
Fashion Flair
Fieldcrest Cannon
Fuller Brush
Gitano
Gitano Children
Hanes Activewear
Hathaway
Ideas
Jonathan Logan
Just My Size
KidsPort USA

Kitchen Collection
Knits by K. T.
Leather Manor
L'eggs/Hanes/Bali
Manhattan
Multiples
Mushrooms
Newport Sportswear
Old Mill
Oneida
OshKosh B'Gosh
Paper Factory
Pfaltzgraff
Pilgrim Glass
Ribbon Outlet
Salem China
Skyr
Sneakers 'n Cleats
Socks Galore
Specials Exclusively by Levi Strauss
Sportsland USA
Sports Wearhouse
Swank Factory Store
Sweatshirt Co.
Tiffany Lamp Factory Outlet
Tool Warehouse
Top of the Line Cosmetics
totes/Sunglass World
Toy Liquidators
TrendSetter Footwear
Van Heusen
Wallet Works
Welcome Home
Winona Knits

Credit Cards: Most stores accept most major credit cards.

Personal Checks: Most stores accept checks with two forms of proper identification.

Handicapped Accessible: Yes

Food: Variety of snacks and foods in mall food court

Bus Tours: Yes

Notes or Attractions: Seven miles from Frankenmuth, where the world's largest Christmas store, Bronner's Christmas Wonderland, is located.

The Village Shops at Birch Run
12158 Beyer Road

Directions: Exit 136 Birch Run/Frankenmuth off I–75
Phone: (517) 624–4846
Hours: 10:00 A.M.–9:00 P.M., Monday–Saturday; 11:00 A.M.–6:00 P.M., Sunday
Outlets:
Adolfo II
American Tourister
Anne Klein
Argenti
Brands
Bruce Alan Bags, Etc.
Capezio
Crystal Works
Eagle's Eye Company Store
E. J. Plum
Etienne Aigner
European Collections/Oleg Cassini
Evan Picone
Fenn Wright & Mason
Gant Company Store
Gilligan O'Malley
harvé benard
J. Crew Factory Store
J. G. Hook Company Store
Jindo Furs
Jones NY Factory Store
Jordache
Just Kids Outlet Store
Kitchen Place

Linen Mill
Liz Claiborne
Maidenform
Mikasa
Nike
Prestige Fragrance
Sassafras
Villeroy & Boch
Wemco
Windsor Shirt Company
Credit Cards: Most stores accept most major credit cards.
Personal Checks: Most stores accept checks with two forms of proper identification.
Handicapped Accessible: Yes
Food: Vending machines in lounge; food court at nearby Manufacturers Marketplace
Bus Tours: Yes

HOLLAND

Manufacturers Marketplace Dutch Village
U.S. 31 and James Street

Directions: I–196 to U.S. 31 at James Street
Phone: (616) 396–1327
Hours: 10:00 A.M.–9:00 P.M., Monday–Saturday; 11:00 A.M.–7:00 P.M., Sunday
Outlets:
Action Housewares Outlet
Aileen
American Tourister
Anko Also
Aunt Mary's Yarns
Banister Shoes

Barbizon Lingerie
Black & Decker
Book Warehouse
Brass Factory Outlet
Bugle Boy
Cape Isle Knitters
Carter's Childrenswear
Clothes Outs
Dress Barn
Eddie Bauer Outlet Store
Famous Designer Outlet
Famous Footwear
Fanny Farmer
Farah Factory Store
Fieldcrest Cannon
Gitano
Hanes Activewear
harvé benard
Hush Puppies
Jonathan Logan
Just About Perfect
KidsPort USA
Kitchen Collection
Knits by K.T.
Leather Manor
Mackintosh of New England
Manhattan
Nickels Company Store
Old Mill
Oneida
Paper Factory
Pfaltzgraff
The Ribbon Outlet
Sneakers-n-Cleats
Socks Galore
Sportsland USA
Sweatshirt Co.
Tanner Factory Store
Tiffany Lamp Factory Outlet

Top of the Line Cosmetics
Toy Liquidators
Van Heusen
Wallet Works
Welcome Home
Winona Knits

Credit Cards: Most stores accept most major credit cards.
Personal Checks: Most stores accept checks with two forms of proper identification.
Handicapped Accessible: Yes
Food: Food court
Bus Tours: Yes
Notes or Attractions: Hotel and theater are located at the mall. Marketplace is adjacent to Holland's Dutch Village, where the annual Tulip Festival is staged. Near the beaches of Lake Michigan.

LIVONIA

Bike Nashbar Factory Outlet Store
19045 Middlebelt Road

Directions: Route 96 to Middlebelt Road exit north, store on left
Phone: (313) 478–1041
Hours: 10:00 A.M.–8:00 P.M., Monday–Friday; 10:00 A.M.–6:00 P.M., Saturday
Credit Cards: Discover, MasterCard, Visa
Personal Checks: Yes, with proper identification
Handicapped Accessible: Yes
Bus Tours: Yes

MONROE

Manufacturers Marketplace
I–75 and LaPlaisance Road

Directions: I–75 to exit 11 North—LaPlaisance Road
Phone: (313) 241–9347
Hours: 10:00 A.M.–9:00 P.M., Monday–Saturday; 11:00 A.M.–7:00 P.M., Sunday
Outlets:
Aileen
American Tourister
Aunt Mary's Yarns
Banister Shoe
Barbizon
Bass Factory Outlet
Book Warehouse
Brass Factory
Cape Isle Knitters
Captree
Carter's Childrenswear
China Plus
Corning/Revere Factory Store
Dress Barn
Famous Designer Outlet
Famous Footwear
Fanny Farmer
Farah Factory Store
Fragrance World
Gitano
Hanes Activewear
harvé benard
Henson-Kickernick
Ideas
Johnston's Fashions for Children
Jordache
Just My Size
Kitchen Collection
Knits by K.T.
Leather Manor
L'eggs/Hanes/Bali
Maidenform
Manhattan
Midway Leather

Multiples
Nilani
Old Mill
Paper Factory
The Ribbon Outlet
Royal Robbins
Salem China
Sneakers-n-Cleats
Socks Galore
Specials Exclusively by Levi Strauss
Sportsland USA
Sports Wearhouse
Stone Mountain Handbags
Swank Factory Outlet
Sweatshirt Co.
Tiffany Lamp Factory Outlet
Tool Warehouse
Top of the Line Cosmetics
Toy Liquidators
Van Heusen
Wallet Works
Welcome Home
Wemco
West Point Pepperell
What A Deal

Credit Cards: Most stores accept most major credit cards.
Personal Checks: Most stores accept checks with two forms of proper identification.
Handicapped Accessible: Yes
Food: Food court plus restaurants
Bus Tours: Yes
Notes or Attractions: Between Toledo and Detroit. Sterling State Park and the Henry Ford Museum are near Detroit, Michigan, and Cedar Point Amusement Park and Boblo Island are close to Toledo, Ohio.

MUSKEGON

Outlets and More Shopping Center
1940 Henry Street

Directions: From Business Route 131, go east on Laketon to Henry Street. Center is between Laketon and Hackley.
Phone: (616) 755–1594
Hours: 10:00 A.M.–9:00 P.M., Monday–Friday; 10:00 A.M.–6:00 P.M., Saturday; noon–5:00 P.M., Sunday
Outlets:
Jaymar-Ruby
KidsPort USA
Little Red Shoe House
Paper Factory
Credit Cards: Most major cards
Personal Checks: Yes
Handicapped Accessible: Yes
Food: Yes
Bus Tours: Yes

ROCKFORD

Rockford Factory Outlet Mall
235 Main Street

Directions: Exit U.S. 131 at Ten Mile Road North
Phone: (616) 866–9100
Hours: 9:00 A.M.–8:00 P.M., Monday–Friday; 9:00 A.M.–6:00 P.M., Saturday; noon–5:00 P.M., Sunday
Outlets:
Brooks Athletic Outlet
Little Red Shoe House

Prestige Fragrance
Van Heusen Factory Outlet
Wallet Works
Winona Knitting Mills
Credit Cards: All major cards
Personal Checks: Yes, with proper identification
Handicapped Accessible: Yes
Food: Available in town approximately 2 blocks away
Bus Tours: Yes

Can't remember what products a particular outlet offers? Check our "Profiles" section beginning on page one. Many listings also contain information on brand names and range of discounts.

MINNESOTA

Numbers to the left of entries in this legend correspond to the numbers on the accompanying map. The number to the right of each city's or town's name is the page number on which that municipality's outlets first appear.

MINNESOTA

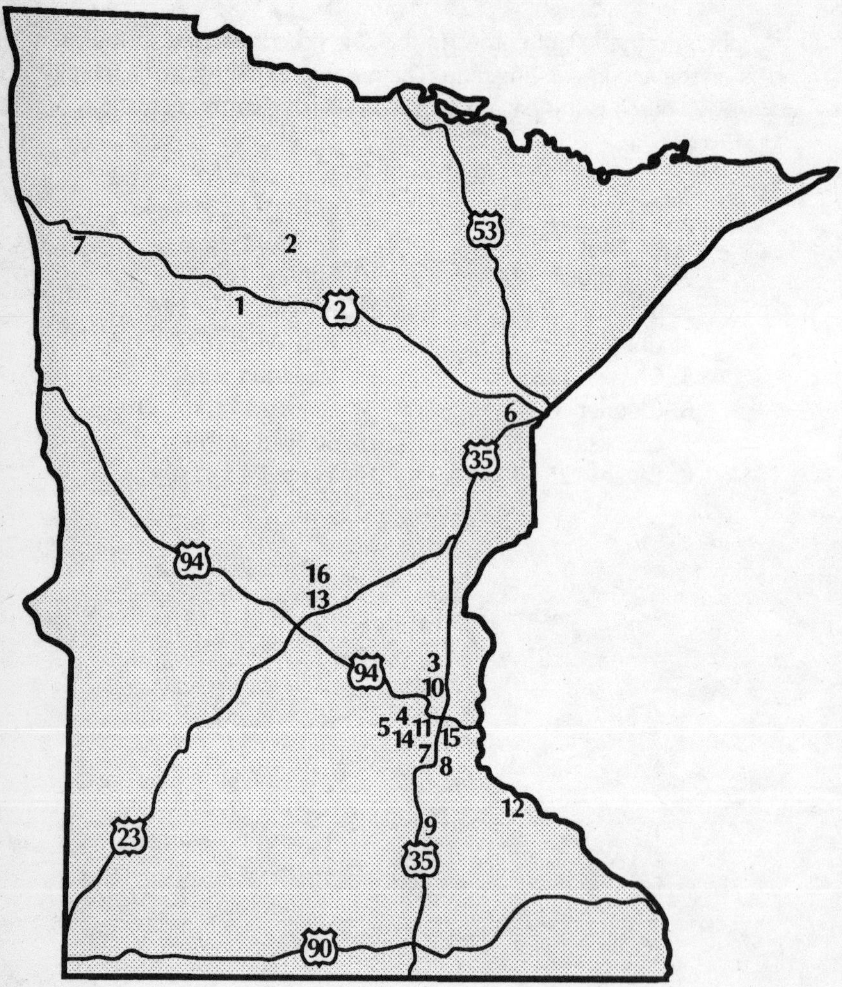

BEMIDJI

Bemidji Woolen Mills, Inc.
301 Irvine Avenue, NW

Directions: At Third Street and Irvine Avenue, 4 blocks west of the statues of Paul Bunyan and Babe the Blue Ox
Phone: (218) 751-5166
Hours: 8:00 A.M.–5:30 P.M., Monday–Saturday
Credit Cards: MasterCard, Visa
Personal Checks: Yes, with proper identification
Handicapped Accessible: Yes
Food: Within walking distance of many restaurants
Bus Tours: Yes
Notes or Attractions: Bemidji is in north-central Minnesota lake country; for factory tours, contact Bill Batchelder.

Lady Slipper Designs
Route 3

Directions: Six miles east of Bemidji on Highway 2 East
Phone: (218) 751-0763; (800) 334-6412
Hours: From Memorial Day to Labor Day, 10:00 A.M.–4:00 P.M., Monday–Friday
Additional Savings: Annual Christmas Sale days—call for dates and hours.
Credit Cards: MasterCard, Visa
Personal Checks: Yes, with proper identification
Handicapped Accessible: Yes
Food: One mile east of outlet
Bus Tours: Yes
Notes or Attractions: Bemidji is the home of statues of Paul Bunyan and Babe the Blue Ox; Itasca Park, at the headwaters of the Mississippi, is 50 miles north.

BLACKDUCK

Anderson Fabrics
Summit Avenue

Directions: North on U.S. 71 from Bemidji, make a right on Summit Avenue, heading for downtown Blackduck.
Phone: (218) 835–6377
Hours: 9:00 A.M.–5:30 P.M., Monday–Friday; 9:00 A.M.–4:00 P.M., Saturday
Credit Cards: MasterCard, Visa
Personal Checks: Yes, with proper identification
Handicapped Accessible: Yes
Food: Within a block
Bus Tours: Yes
Notes or Attractions: Factory tour can be arranged by contacting store manager. Near Chippewa National Forest, Bemidji is 25 miles south.

BLAINE

Sears Surplus
9056 Penn Avenue South

Directions: Take 90th or 94th Street exit off Highway 35W for roughly 5 blocks west, 1 mile south of Southtown Shopping Mall.
Phone: (612) 884–5317
Hours: 10:00 A.M.–6:00 P.M., Monday–Saturday; during Christmas, 10:00 A.M.–9:00 P.M., Monday–Saturday, and 10:00 A.M.–6:00 P.M., Sunday
Credit Cards: Discover, Sears
Personal Checks: Yes, with proper identification
Handicapped Accessible: Yes
Food: Fast food next door
Bus Tours: Yes

CHANHASSEN

Carousel Animal Fair Factory Outlet Store
581 W. 78th Street

Directions: Call ahead.
Phone: (612) 934–0444
Hours: 9:00 A.M.–4:30 P.M., Monday–Friday
Credit Cards: No
Personal Checks: Yes
Handicapped Accessible: Yes
Food: Within 2 blocks
Bus Tours: Yes

CHASKA

Minnetonka Factory Outlet
110650 Village Road

Directions: From I–94, exit at 11C and go west approximately 8 miles on Highway 5 to Highway 41; turn left, go 2.6 miles south to Johnson Boulevard, turn right, and follow signs.
Phone: For current hours, specials, and directions, (612) 448–6900 or The Connection, (612) 922–9000.
Hours: 9:00 A.M.–5:00 P.M., Monday–Friday; 10:00 A.M.–5:00 P.M., Saturday. For Sunday and seasonal hours, call The Connection.
Credit Cards: American Express, MasterCard, Visa
Personal Checks: Only from Minnesota residents
Handicapped Accessible: Yes
Food: Within 5 miles, there is a variety from fast food to fine dining.
Bus Tours: Yes, one-week advance notice preferred. Usually a small gift is provided to tour guests.
Notes or Attractions: Close to Valleyfair family amusement park, Canterbury Downs Racetrack, and Murphy's Landing living history center.

CLOQUET

Bergquist Imports, Inc.
1412 Highway 33 South

Directions: Take I–35 to Cloquet and get off at the Highway 33 exit. Outlet is ½ mile from exit.
Phone: (218) 879–1142
Hours: 9:00 A.M.–5:30 P.M., Monday–Saturday
Credit Cards: Most major cards
Personal Checks: Yes
Handicapped Accessible: Yes
Food: Restaurants and fast food within a 1-mile radius
Bus Tours: Yes
Notes or Attractions: Cloquet is near Dunlop Island, which features a western fort and an Indian village. Bergquist Imports has a gift shop on the premises that offers the largest selection of Scandinavian gift items in the United States.

CROOKSTON

Anderson Fabrics
109 S. Broadway

Directions: U.S. 2 West from Bemidji to Crookston exit (Broadway).
Phone: (218) 281–1806
Hours: 9:30 A.M.–6:00 P.M., Monday–Wednesday, Friday; 9:30 A.M.–9:00 P.M., Thursday; 9:30 A.M.–5:00 P.M., Saturday; noon–4:00 P.M., Sunday
Credit Cards: MasterCard, Visa
Personal Checks: Yes, with proper identification
Handicapped Accessible: Yes
Food: Within a block
Bus Tours: Yes
Notes or Attractions: Near scenic Red River Valley area

EAGAN

Recie's Sample Shop
1975 Seneca Road

Directions: Highway 13 between Yankee Doodle Road and Cedar (close to St. Paul and Minneapolis)
Phone: (612) 454–7720
Hours: 10:00 A.M.–5:30 P.M., Monday, Tuesday, Friday, Saturday; 10:00 A.M.–9:00 P.M., Wednesday, Thursday; noon–5:00 P.M., Sunday
Additional Savings: Sales after Christmas and July 4
Credit Cards: Discover, MasterCard, Visa
Personal Checks: Yes
Handicapped Accessible: Yes
Food: Two blocks from store
Bus Tours: Yes

FARIBAULT

Faribo Woolens Factory Store
1819 W. Second Avenue

Directions: Take I–35 to Faribault; then follow billboards.
Phone: (507) 334–1644
Hours: 9:00 A.M.–5:30 P.M., Monday–Saturday; noon–4:00 P.M., Sunday
Additional Savings: June clearance, January clearance, and fall festival
Credit Cards: American Express, MasterCard, Visa
Personal Checks: Yes, with proper identification
Handicapped Accessible: Yes
Food: One mile away
Bus Tours: Yes

FRIDLEY

Sears Surplus
1000 N.E. East Moore Lake Drive

Directions: One mile north of Highway 694 on Highway 65
Phone: (612) 571–8010
Hours: 9:00 A.M.–9:00 P.M., Monday–Saturday; 10:00 A.M.–6:00 P.M., Sunday
Credit Cards: Discover, Sears
Personal Checks: Yes, with proper identification
Handicapped Accessible: Yes
Food: Available in the area
Bus Tours: Yes

MINNEAPOLIS

Dayton's Outlet Store
701 Industrial Boulevard

Directions: Take 35W to exit 22; proceed 2 blocks to Industrial Boulevard, close to Rosedale Mall.
Phone: (612) 623–7111
Hours: 9:30 A.M.–9:30 P.M., Monday–Friday; 9:30 A.M.–6:00 P.M., Saturday; noon–6:00 P.M., Sunday
Credit Cards: American Express, Dayton's, Discover, MasterCard, Visa
Personal Checks: Yes, with driver's license or Dayton's charge
Handicapped Accessible: Yes
Food: In the vicinity
Bus Tours: Yes

Eddie Bauer Outlet Store
821 Marquette Avenue

Directions: Take I–35W to Fifth Avenue exit; go 1 block and make a

left at S. Ninth Street; continue to Marquette Avenue and make a right. Store is on right-hand side between S. Eighth and S. Seventh streets.
Phone: (612) 341–0504
Hours: 9:30 A.M.–6:00 P.M., Monday–Friday; 9:30 A.M.–5:30 P.M., Saturday; noon–5:00 P.M., Sunday
Credit Cards: American Express, Eddie Bauer Charger, MasterCard, Visa
Personal Checks: Yes, with proper identification
Handicapped Accessible: Yes
Food: All around downtown area

Sears Outlet Store
2700 N.E. Winter Street

Directions: West of Highway 280 on Hennepin Avenue, south of Industrial Boulevard and Hennepin
Phone: (612) 379–5600
Hours: 9:00 A.M.–9:00 P.M., Monday–Friday; 9:00 A.M.–5:00 P.M., Saturday, noon–5:00 P.M., Sunday
Credit Cards: All major cards
Personal Checks: Yes, with two forms of proper identification and driver's license showing date of birth
Handicapped Accessible: Yes
Food: Within a few blocks
Bus Tours: Yes

RED WING

Pottery Place Factory Outlet Mall
2000 W. Main Street

Directions: Withers Harbor Drive exit off Highway 61
Phone: (612) 388–8385
Hours: 9:00 A.M.–8:00 P.M., Monday–Friday; 9:00 A.M.–6:00 P.M., Saturday; 11:00 A.M.–6:00 P.M., Sunday

Outlets:
Aileen
Banister Shoes
Bass Shoe Outlet
Benetton
Clothesworks
Corning/Revere Factory Store
Great Lakes Trading Company
Little Red Shoe House
Munsingwear Factory Outlet
Plums Sweaters for Less
Prestige Fragrance & Cosmetics
The Ribbon Outlet
Sylvester's Fashion Outlet
Van Heusen
Vassarette
Wallet Works
Winona Glove Sales
The Woolen Mill
Credit Cards: Most stores accept major credit cards.
Personal Checks: Most stores accept checks with two forms of proper identification.
Handicapped Accessible: Yes
Food: Two casual restaurants and two snack-food vendors in building
Bus Tours: Yes
Notes or Attractions: One hour south of Minneapolis/St. Paul. Red Wing is a mid-nineteenth-century Mississippi River town with restored historic buildings.

ST. CLOUD

American Bicycle Manufacturing
3102 Roosevelt Road

Directions: From I–94, take the Highway 75 exit (Augusta/St. Cloud); go west at 25th Avenue.

Phone: (612) 251–1641
Hours: 8:00 A.M.–5:00 P.M., Monday–Friday
Credit Cards: No
Personal Checks: Yes
Handicapped Accessible: Yes
Food: Restaurants and fast food within 2 blocks
Bus Tours: Yes

Jennings Decoy Company
601 Franklin Avenue, NE

Directions: From I–94, take Highway 15 North to Highway 23 East, or take Division Street to Highway 10 East, turn left on East St. Germain, turn right on frontage road (Franklin Avenue).
Phone: (612) 253–2253
Hours: 8:00 A.M.–5:00 P.M., Monday–Friday; 9:00 A.M.–12:00 P.M., Saturday
Credit Cards: Most major cards
Personal Checks: Yes
Handicapped Accessible: Yes
Food: Restaurants and fast food across the street
Bus Tours: Yes

ST. LOUIS PARK

Burlington Coat Factory Warehouse
3700 S. Highway 100

Directions: Call ahead.
Phone: (612) 929–6850
Hours: 10:00 A.M.–9:00 P.M., Monday–Saturday; noon–5:00 P.M., Sunday
Credit Cards: MasterCard, Visa

Personal Checks: Yes, with proper identification
Handicapped Accessible: Yes
Food: Available on Highway 100

ST. PAUL

Milbern Clothing Co.
two locations:
1685 University Avenue (Midway area), 2 blocks east of Snelling and University avenues; (612) 645–2922
Galtier Plaza, 2nd floor (Milton Division), in downtown St. Paul; (612) 224–6443

Hours: Midway—9:00 A.M.–5:00 P.M., Tuesday, Wednesday, Friday, Saturday; 9:00 A.M.–9:00 P.M., Monday and Thursday; Milton Division—10:00 A.M.–7:00 P.M., Monday–Saturday; noon–5:00 P.M., Sunday
Additional Savings: Warehouse clearance—call for dates.
Credit Cards: Discover, MasterCard, Visa
Personal Checks: Yes
Handicapped Accessible: Yes
Food: Available nearby

WAITE PARK

The Dollar Super Store
210 Third Street North

Directions: From I–94, take Highway 15 North to Highway 23 West.
Phone: (612) 253–2500
Hours: 10:00 A.M.–9:00 P.M., Monday–Friday; 9:00 A.M.–6:00 P.M., Saturday; noon–6:00 P.M., Sunday
Credit Cards: No
Personal Checks: Yes
Handicapped Accessible: Yes
Food: Restaurants and fast food within ½ mile
Bus Tours: Yes

MISSOURI

Numbers to the left of entries in this legend correspond to the numbers on the accompanying map. The number to the right of each city's or town's name is the page number on which that municipality's outlets first appear.

MISSOURI

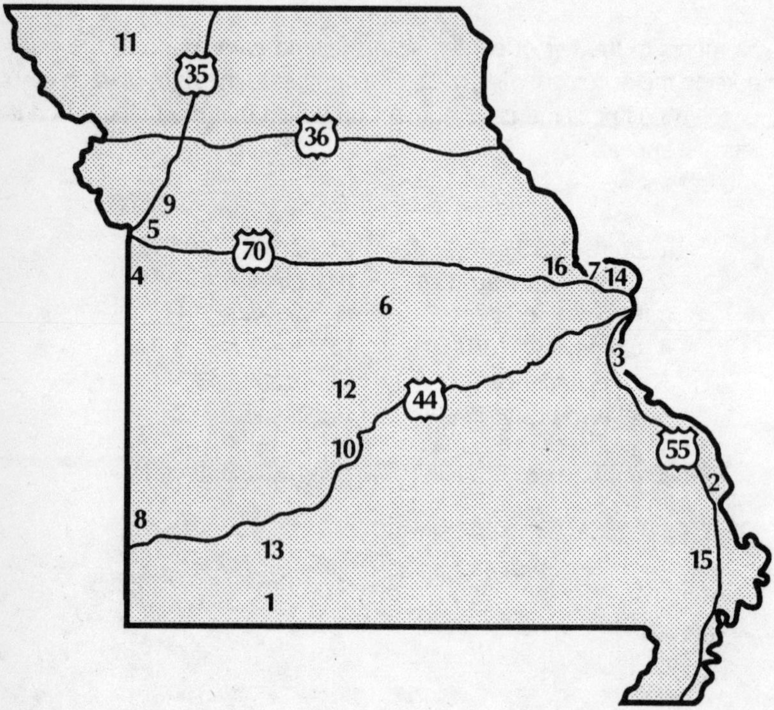

BRANSON

Factory Merchants Mall of Branson
1000 Pat Nash Drive

Directions: U.S. 65 to Shepherd of the Hills Bypass to Gretna Road, off Highway 76.
Phone: (417) 335–6686
Hours: April to December—9:00 A.M.–8:00 P.M., Monday–Saturday; 9:00 A.M.–6:00 P.M., Sunday; January to March—10:00 A.M.–6:00 P.M., every day
Outlets:
Aileen Factory Outlet
American Tourister
Banister Shoes
Barbizon Lingerie
Bass Shoes
Book Warehouse
Bruce Alan Bags, Etc.
Campus
Cape Isle Knitters
Carter's Childrenswear
Corning Factory Store
Dunn Woodcrafters
Evan Picone Factory Store
Famous Footwear
Fashion Flair
Fieldcrest Cannon
Full Size Fashion
Gitano
harvé benard
Jaymar Factory Outlet
Jonathan Logan Outlet
Kitchen Collection, Inc.
The Leather Factory
Little Red Shoe House
London Fog Factory Store
Manhattan
Mushroom Shoes

Oneida Factory Outlet
OshKosh B'Gosh
Paul Revere Shoppe
Pfaltzgraff
Polly Flinders
Prestige Fragrances
Rawlings
The Ribbon Outlet
Sans Souci Lingerie
Socks Galore & More
Tanner Factory Store
This Gift's For You
totes/Sunglass World
Toys Unlimited
Van Heusen Factory Store
Vermillion Factory Outlet
The Wallet Works
Welcome Home
Credit Cards: Most major cards
Personal Checks: Most merchants accept checks with proper identification.
Handicapped Accessible: Yes
Food: Deli, salad bar, and frozen yogurt in mall
Bus Tours: Yes, ample parking
Notes or Attractions: In Ozark Mountain country, a vacation getaway with attractions for the entire family

CAPE GIRARDEAU

Florsheim Shoe Factory Outlet
48 Plaza Way

Directions: Two blocks east of I–55 (exit 96) at 48 Plaza Way
Phone: (314) 334–9544
Hours: 9:00 A.M.–5:30 P.M., Monday–Saturday; 1:00–5:00 P.M., Sunday (summer only)

Credit Cards: American Express, Discover, MasterCard, Visa
Personal Checks: Yes, out-of-state residents need drivers' license identification.
Handicapped Accessible: Yes
Food: A variety of restaurants within 2 miles
Bus Tours: Yes

Thorngate Ltd. Slack Outlet
637 Broadway

Directions: Take Route K exit off I–55; go left on Sprigg, then right onto Broadway.
Phone: (314) 651–3130
Hours: 9:00 A.M.–5:00 P.M., Monday–Friday; 9:00 A.M.–4:00 P.M., Saturday
Credit Cards: MasterCard, Visa
Personal Checks: Yes, with proper identification
Handicapped Accessible: Yes
Food: A variety of restaurants within 2 miles

Warehouse of Leathers
261 West Park Mall

Directions: Route K exit off I–55
Phone: (314) 335–3333
Hours: 10:00 A.M.–9:30 P.M., Monday–Saturday; 12:30–5:30 P.M., Sunday
Credit Cards: American Express, Discover, MasterCard, Visa
Personal Checks: Yes, with driver's license (with photograph) and major credit card
Handicapped Accessible: Yes
Food: Restaurants in the mall
Bus Tours: Yes
Notes or Attractions: Several miles from scenic, French-style waterfront in downtown Cape Girardeau and Trail of Tears State Park.

FESTUS

Florsheim Shoe Factory Outlet
1159 Gannon Drive

Directions: Call ahead.
Phone: (314) 933–5153
Hours: 9:00 A.M.–5:30 P.M., Monday–Saturday
Credit Cards: American Express, Discover, MasterCard, Visa
Personal Checks: Yes, with driver's license identification for out-of-state residents
Handicapped Accessible: Yes

GRANDVIEW

Montgomery Ward Clearance
12344 S. 71 Highway

Directions: Blue Ridge Boulevard exit off 71 Highway
Phone: (816) 765–4431
Hours: 10:00 A.M.–8:00 P.M., Monday–Friday; 10:00 A.M.–6:00 P.M., Saturday; noon–5:00 P.M., Sunday
Credit Cards: American Express, Discover, MasterCard, Visa, Ward's
Personal Checks: Yes, with proper identification
Handicapped Accessible: Yes
Food: Fast food nearby
Bus Tours: Yes
Notes or Attractions: Behind farm home of Harry S Truman.

Shoe Cents
12144 S. 71 Highway

Directions: Blue Ridge Boulevard exit off 71 Highway to Truman Corners Shopping Center
Phone: (816) 763–1611

Hours: 10:00 A.M.–9:00 P.M., Monday–Saturday; noon–5:00 P.M., Sunday
Additional Savings: Seasonal sales in July, August, February, and March
Credit Cards: Discover, MasterCard, Visa
Personal Checks: Yes, with valid driver's license
Handicapped Accessible: Yes
Food: Fast food nearby
Notes or Attractions: Harry S Truman farm home 2 blocks away

INDEPENDENCE

Drug Emporium
2341 S. Highway 291

Directions: Three miles north of I–70 on Highway 291
Phone: (816) 373–4550
Hours: 9:00 A.M.–9:00 P.M., Monday–Saturday; 10:00 A.M.–6:00 P.M., Sunday
Credit Cards: MasterCard, Visa
Personal Checks: Yes, with driver's license, address, and telephone number
Handicapped Accessible: Yes
Food: Available in the neighborhood
Bus Tours: Yes
Notes or Attractions: Near Truman Library

Half Price Store
13500 "A" E. 40 Highway

Directions: Six blocks south of I–70 at Noland Fashion Square, 40 Highway and Noland Road
Phone: (816) 478–1800
Hours: 9:00 A.M.–10:00 P.M., daily; extended hours during Christmas season

Additional Savings: January and July clearance sales
Credit Cards: Discover, MasterCard, Richman Gordman, Visa
Personal Checks: Yes, with driver's license
Handicapped Accessible: Yes, with a wheelchair available
Food: Available nearby
Bus Tours: Yes

Underwriters Sales Outlet
13900 E. 35th Street

Directions: I–70 to Noland Road exit, north. Go 7 blocks on Noland Road to 35th Street; turn left on 35th Street for ½ block.
Phone: (816) 252–9666
Hours: 10:00 A.M.–5:00 P.M., Tuesday, Wednesday, Friday; 10:00 A.M.–8:00 P.M., Thursday; 10:00 A.M.–4:00 P.M., Saturday
Additional Savings: Spring and fall sales
Credit Cards: MasterCard, Visa
Personal Checks: No checks under $10.00
Handicapped Accessible: Yes

JEFFERSON CITY

Florsheim Shoe Factory Store
12 Wilson Drive

Directions: Call ahead.
Phone: (314) 635–1210
Hours: 9:00 A.M.–5:30 P.M., Monday–Saturday
Credit Cards: American Express, Discover, MasterCard, Visa
Personal Checks: Yes. Out-of-state checks require driver's license identification.
Handicapped Accessible: Yes

JENNINGS

J. C. Penney Catalog Outlet Store
Number 55 at River Road Mall

Directions: Halls Ferry Road at Jennings Station Road
Phone: (314) 868–9700
Hours: 9:30 A.M.–9:30 P.M., Monday–Saturday, 11:00 A.M.–6:00 P.M., Sunday
Credit Cards: American Express, J. C. Penney, MasterCard, Visa
Personal Checks: Yes, with valid driver's license or major credit card
Handicapped Accessible: Yes
Food: Within the mall
Bus Tours: Yes

JOPLIN

Florsheim Shoe Factory Outlet
102 Range Line Road

Directions: Call ahead.
Phone: (417) 782–8577
Hours: 9:00 A.M.–5:30 P.M., Monday–Saturday
Credit Cards: American Express, Discover, MasterCard, Visa
Personal Checks: Yes. Out-of-state checks require driver's license identification.
Handicapped Accessible: Yes

KANSAS CITY

Kuppenheimer Men's Clothiers
55 Blue Ridge Mall, 4200 Blue Ridge Boulevard

Directions: I–70 to Blue Ridge Boulevard. Turn right from the highway into Blue Ridge Mall.

Phone: (816) 353–6307
Hours: 10:00 A.M.–9:00 P.M., Monday–Saturday; noon–5:30 P.M., Sunday
Additional Savings: January and July clearance sales
Credit Cards: American Express, Discover, MasterCard, Visa
Personal Checks: Yes, for state residents with major credit-card identification; no out-of-state checks
Handicapped Accessible: Yes
Food: In the mall
Bus Tours: Ample mall parking
Notes or Attractions: Within an hour of Worlds of Fun and downtown Kansas City; close to the Plaza and West Port tourist areas

LEBANON

VF Factory Outlet Mall
2020 Industrial Drive

Directions: Take I–44 to exit 129 (Highway 5 South). Turn right on Lawson Avenue to Market Street, then left into VF Factory Outlet Mall.
Phone: (417) 588–4142
Hours: 10:00 A.M.–7:00 P.M., Monday–Saturday
Additional Savings: End-of-season clearance, Presidents Day, and Independence Day sales
Outlets:
American Tourister
Banister
Evan Picone Factory Store
Jonathan Logan
The Paper Factory
Prestige Fragrances & Cosmetics
Reading Bag
totes
Van Heusen Factory Store
VF Factory Outlet
Your Toy Center

Credit Cards: MasterCard, Visa
Personal Checks: Yes, with photograph identification
Handicapped Accessible: Yes
Food: Snack bar at mall, restaurants nearby
Bus Tours: Yes; complimentary coffee and snack for tour leader and bus driver
Notes or Attractions: Trout fishing, camping, and canoeing in Bennett Springs resort area

MARYVILLE

Slightly Imperfix
202 E. Third Street

Directions: Southeast corner of Courthouse Square
Phone: (816) 582–4660
Hours: 10:00 A.M.–5:00 P.M., Monday–Saturday
Additional Savings: July sidewalk and December Christmas sales with 20 percent off storewide
Credit Cards: No
Personal Checks: Yes
Handicapped Accessible: Yes
Food: Available 1 mile away

OSAGE BEACH

Osage Village Factory Merchants Etc.
Route 54

Directions: Route 54, near Route 42 in the center of Osage Beach
Phone: (314) 348–2065
Hours: April to December—9:00 A.M.–9:00 P.M., Monday–Saturday; 9:00 A.M.–6:00 P.M., Sunday; January to March—10:00 A.M.–6:00 P.M., daily

Outlets:
Aileen Factory Outlet
Anne Klein
Banister Shoes
Bruce Alan Bags, Etc.
Campus
Capezio Shoe
Carter's Childrenswear
Clothesworks by Jack Winter
Corning Factory Store
Dansk
Evan Picone Factory Store
Factory Shoe Outlet
Gant Company Store
GeGe's
The Genuine Article
G. H. Bass
Grey Goose
Hanes Activewear
harvé benard
Henson Lingerie Factory Store
Izod Company Store
Jaymar Factory Outlet
J. G. Hook Company Store
Jonathan Logan
Kitchen Collection
Leggoons Sportswear
L'eggs/Hanes/Bali
London Fog Factory Store
Manhattan Factory Store
Nike Factory Outlet
Oneida Factory Store
Paul Revere Shoppe
Polly Flinders
Polo/Ralph Lauren
Prestige Cosmetics
The Ribbon Outlet, Inc.
Skyr
totes

Toys Unlimited
Van Heusen
The Wallet Works
Warnaco
Credit Cards: Most major cards accepted
Personal Checks: Most stores accept checks with proper identification
Handicapped Accessible: Yes
Food: Located within the mall
Bus Tours: Ample parking in lot
Notes or Attractions: In the heart of the Missouri Ozarks at Lake of the Ozarks, a family and convention vacation destination

OZARK

Native Wood Products
Highway 14 and Business 65

Directions: At the stoplight where Highway 14 and Business 65 intersect
Phone: (417) 485-6683
Hours: 8:00 A.M.–5:00 P.M., Monday–Friday; 9:00 A.M.–5:00 P.M., Saturday, Sunday, holidays; closed weekends Thanksgiving through Easter
Credit Cards: Discover, MasterCard, Visa
Personal Checks: Yes
Handicapped Accessible: Yes
Food: Available on the block
Bus Tours: Yes, ample parking
Notes or Attractions: In Ozark Mountain country vacation area

ST. LOUIS

Shoe Stop
20 Plaza St. Clair (Fairview Heights)

Directions: Call ahead.
Phone: (314) 632–8909
Hours: 10:00 A.M.–8:30 P.M., daily
Additional Savings: Final clearance sales at the end of each season
Credit Cards: American Express, Discover, MasterCard, Visa
Personal Checks: Yes, preprinted checks with valid driver's license identification; no starter checks
Handicapped Accessible: Yes
Bus Tours: Yes

SIKESTON

London Fog Factory Stores
Village Green Shopping Center

Directions: Call ahead.
Phone: (314) 472–1766
Hours: 10:00 A.M.–9:00 P.M., Monday–Saturday; noon–5:00 P.M., Sunday
Credit Cards: MasterCard, Visa
Personal Checks: Yes, with major credit card, driver's license, and name of employer
Handicapped Accessible: Yes
Bus Tours: Ample parking lot

WENTZVILLE

Belz Factory Outlet Mall
100 Mall Parkway

Directions: Take exit 212A off I–70.

Phone: (314) 327–8110
Hours: 10:00 A.M.–9:00 A.M., Monday–Saturday; noon–6:00 P.M., Sunday
Outlets:
Amy Stoudt
Bag & Baggage
Banister Shoe Outlet
Bookland
Burlington Coat Factory Warehouse
Burlington Shoe Store
Coffee Boutique
Crown Jewels
Dress Barn
Famous Footwear
Famous Name Gifts
Fieldcrest Cannon (Beacon Linens)
Frontier Fruit & Nut
Gitano
Gold Connection
Jewelies
Kitchen Collection
L'eggs/Hanes/Bali
Mikasa Factory Store
Music Vision
Old Mill Ladies Sportswear
Old Time Pottery
Plumm's
Reading Shoes
Regal
The Ribbon Outlet
Top of the Line Cosmetics
Toy Liquidators
Credit Cards: Most major cards
Personal Checks: Most merchants accept checks with proper identification
Handicapped Accessible: Stores on one level
Food: Food court located within the mall
Bus Tours: Yes

OHIO

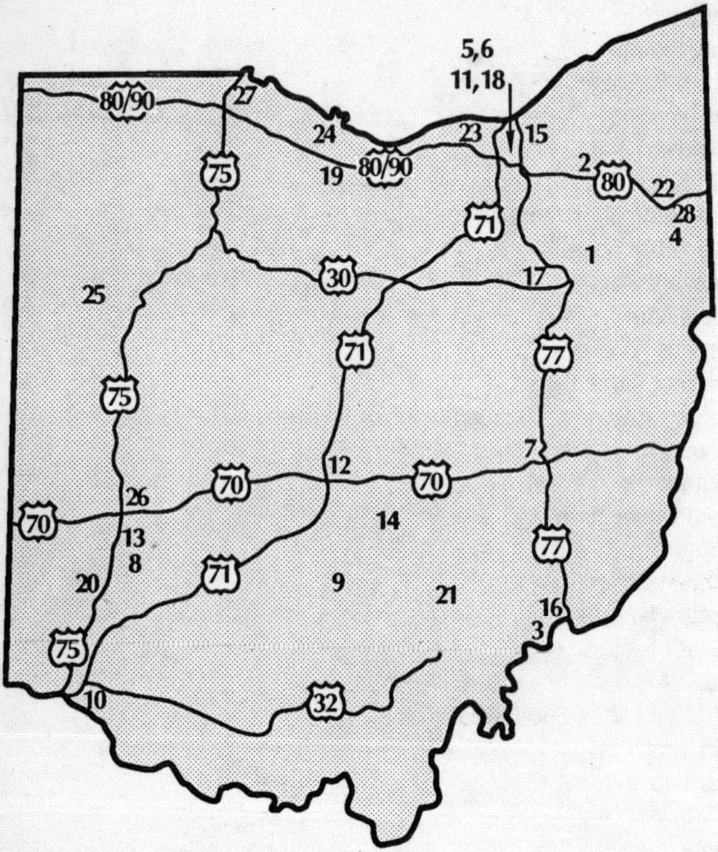
5,6
11,18
27
80/90
24
23
15
75
19
80/90
2
80
22
28
4
71
1
17
30
25
71
77
75
7
12
70
70
26
70
13
8
20
71
14
9
21
77
16
3
75
10
32

OHIO

Numbers to the left of entries in this legend correspond to the numbers on the accompanying map. The number to the right of each city's or town's name is the page number on which that municipality's outlets first appear.

ALLIANCE

El-Bee Shoe Outlets
2500 W. State Street

Directions: From Route 62, go ½ mile east on Route 173 to Carnation Mall.
Phone: (216) 821–1120
Hours: 10:00 A.M.–9:00 P.M., Monday–Saturday; noon–5:00 P.M., Sunday
Credit Cards: American Express, Discover, Elder-Beerman, MasterCard, Visa
Personal Checks: Yes
Handicapped Accessible: Partial
Food: Fast food nearby and in mall
Bus Tours: Yes

Sherwood Coats of Ohio
45 North Arch Street

Directions: In downtown Alliance near routes 62, 183, and 225
Phone: (216) 823–4020
Hours: 10:00 A.M.–4:00 P.M., Monday–Saturday; closed Saturday in June, July, and August
Credit Cards: Most major cards
Personal Checks: Yes
Handicapped Accessible: Yes
Food: Nearby in downtown area
Bus Tours: Yes

AURORA

Aurora Farms Factory Outlet
549 S. Chillicothe Road

Directions: Route 43, 1 mile south of Route 82

Phone: (216) 562–2000 or (800) 837–2001
Hours: 10:00 A.M.–6:00 P.M., Monday–Wednesday; 10:00 A.M.–9:00 P.M., Thursday–Saturday; 10:00 A.M.–5:00 P.M., Sunday
Outlets:
Aileen
American Tourister
Banister Shoes
Bass Shoes
Campus Factory Outlet
Cape Isle Knitters
Carlson's Christmas Collection
Carter's Childrenswear
Corning/Revere Ware
Crazy Horse
Gitano
Hanes Activewear
harvé benard
The Housewares Store
Jonathan Logan Outlet
Jones New York Factory Store
Leather Loft Stores
L'eggs/Hanes/Bali
Manhattan Factory Outlet
The Paper Factory
Prestige Fragrance & Cosmetics, Inc.
The Ribbon Outlet
Salem China
Sequels Book Outlet
Sports Wearhouse
Van Heusen Factory Outlet
The Wallet Works
Wayside Workshop
Welcome Home
Credit Cards: Most stores accept all major credit cards.
Personal Checks: Most stores accept personal checks.
Handicapped Accessible: Yes
Food: Restaurant and snack shops on premises
Bus Tours: Yes, coupon brochure featuring additional savings for groups; bus driver and escort receive a "$5.00 coin" redeemable at stores or eateries

Notes or Attractions: Minutes away from Sea World, Geauga Lake, and Cuyahoga Valley National Recreation Park; year-round flea market and farmers market held every Wednesday and Sunday

BELPRE

Middleton Doll Factory Outlet
1301 Washington Boulevard

Directions: Take I–77 to 7 South to Belpre exit; factory is 3 miles on left from exit.
Phone: (614) 423–1481
Hours: 10:00 A.M.–5:00 P.M., Monday–Saturday
Credit Cards: MasterCard, Visa
Personal Checks: Yes, with proper identification
Handicapped Accessible: Yes
Food: Nearby
Bus Tours: Yes
Notes or Attractions: Free factory tours by appointment. If wheelchair-bound, request factory tour when bus groups aren't scheduled.

BOARDMAN

B & J Sales
7050 Market Street

Directions: One block north of Southern Park Mall next to Boardman Beauty School
Phone: (216) 726–0010
Hours: 10:00 A.M.–6:00 P.M., Monday–Saturday, plus extended holiday hours
Additional Savings: Specials run for all holidays.

Credit Cards: Discover, MasterCard, Visa
Personal Checks: Yes, with proper identification
Handicapped Accessible: Yes
Food: Next door
Bus Tours: Yes

BROOKLYN

Cricketeer For Her
4600 Tiedeman Road

Directions: I–480 to exit 13 (Tiedeman Road). Go ½ mile north; warehouse is on left-hand side.
Phone: (216) 941–3323
Hours: 11:00 A.M.–6:00 P.M., Wednesday; 11:00 A.M.–8:00 P.M., Thursday and Friday; 9:00 A.M.–5:00 P.M., Saturday; 11:00 A.M.–5:00 P.M., Sunday
Additional Savings: Seasonal closeout sales in June and December
Credit Cards: MasterCard, Visa
Personal Checks: Yes, with driver's license
Handicapped Accessible: Yes
Food: Fast food and restaurants ¾ mile from warehouse
Bus Tours: Yes

BROOK PARK

American Commodore Tuxedo
Brookgate Shopping Center
5847 Smith Road

Directions: Located at intersection of Rockside and Smith roads
Phone: (216) 676–6050

Hours: 10:00 A.M.–6:00 P.M., Monday–Saturday
Additional Savings: Spring and fall sales
Credit Cards: American Express, Diners Club, Discover, MasterCard, Visa
Personal Checks: Yes, with an Ohio driver's license and major credit card; no out-of-state checks
Handicapped Accessible: Yes
Food: Available nearby
Bus Tours: Yes
Notes or Attractions: Near Parmatown Mall

CAMBRIDGE

Boyd's Crystal Art Glass
1203 Morton Avenue

Directions: Exit at Cambridge, Route 209 North, from I–70 to Woodlawn Avenue; then turn left at Morton.
Phone: (614) 439–2077
Hours: 8:00 A.M.–4:00 P.M., daily; during June, July, and August, 9:00 A.M.–4:00 P.M., Saturday
Credit Cards: MasterCard, Visa
Personal Checks: Yes, with proper identification
Handicapped Accessible: Limited; call ahead for information.
Food: Fast food nearby
Bus Tours: Yes; notify prior to visit.
Notes or Attractions: Free glass-making factory tours

Factory Glass, Candle & Gift Outlet
2029 Southgate Parkway

Directions: From exit 178 off I–70, take 209 North till Rax Restaurant; turn right into the Deer Creek Motel complex.
Phone: (614) 432–6391 ext. 109 (candle), ext. 105 (glass)

Hours: 9:00 A.M.–5:00 P.M., daily; Memorial Day through Labor Day, 9:00 A.M.–8:00 P.M., daily; closed January through March
Credit Cards: MasterCard, Visa
Personal Checks: Yes, with proper identification and driver's license; prefer numbered checks above 500 unless local
Handicapped Accessible: One step up, aisles wide enough for wheelchairs
Food: Restaurants and fast food close by
Bus Tours: Yes

CENTERVILLE

El-bee Shoe Outlets
1041 Lebanon Pike

Directions: From exit 44 off I–75, go left at light onto Route 725 (Miamisburg–Centerville Road). At Route 48 (Main Street), go right. Store is in Centerville Place in 2 miles.
Phone: (513) 433–6995
Hours: 10:00 A.M.–9:00 P.M., Monday–Saturday; noon–5:00 P.M., Sunday
Credit Cards: American Express, Discover, Elder-Beerman, MasterCard, Visa
Personal Checks: Yes
Handicapped Accessible: Partial
Food: Fast food nearby
Bus Tours: Yes

Hit or Miss
Crosspointe Shopping Center
Alexandersville-Bellbrook Road

Directions: Call ahead.

Phone: (513) 435–4894
Hours: 10:00 A.M.–9:00 P.M., Monday–Saturday; noon–5:00 P.M., Sunday
Additional Savings: Merchandise frequently marked down
Credit Cards: American Express, Discover, MasterCard, Visa
Personal Checks: Yes, from banks within a 60-mile radius
Handicapped Accessible: Yes
Food: In shopping center
Bus Tours: Yes

CHILLICOTHE

El-Bee Shoe Outlets
Bridge Street

Directions: Take Route 35 East to U.S. 23 (Bridge Street) and turn left into Chillicothe Mall.
Phone: (614) 773–3844
Hours: 10:00 A.M.–9:00 P.M., Monday–Saturday; noon–5:00 P.M., Sunday
Credit Cards: American Express, Discover, Elder-Beerman, MasterCard, Visa
Personal Checks: Yes
Handicapped Accessible: Partial
Food: Fast food nearby
Bus Tours: Yes

Kitchen Collection Factory Outlet Store
71 E. Water Street

Directions: Call ahead.
Phone: (614) 773–9150
Hours: 10:00 A.M.–9:00 P.M., Monday–Saturday; noon–6:00 P.M., Sunday
Additional Savings: Monthly sales

Credit Cards: Discover, MasterCard, Visa
Personal Checks: Yes, with driver's license or photo identification
Handicapped Accessible: Yes
Food: Along Route 33
Bus Tours: Yes, 10 percent discount to bus groups

CINCINNATI

El-Bee Shoe Outlets
nine locations:
565 Forest Fair Mall—I–75 to I–275 to Forest Park exit; right off exit to shopping center; (513) 671–7666
3224 Highland Avenue—I–71 to Ridge Avenue exit; left off exit; Highland Ridge shopping center on right; (513) 351–2413
8000 Beechmont Avenue—I–275 to Beechmont exit; Cherry Grove Plaza ½ mile on right; (513) 528–4166
11959 Route 42—I–275 to Sharonville exit (Route 42); left off exit to K-Mart shopping center; (513) 563–0649
5704 Harrison Road—I–74 to Rybolt Road; left off exit, right onto Harrison Road; K-Mart shopping center 5 miles on left; (513) 574–1496
8437 Colerain Pike—I–275 to Colerain Avenue exit; left at light; Colerain Hills shopping center 2 miles on right; (513) 741–7155
3764 Paxton Road—I–71 to Ridge Avenue exit; left off exit, then left onto Ridge Avenue, right on Paxton; Hyde Park shopping center on left; (513) 231–3355
7387 Kenwood Road—I–71 to Montgomery Road exit; right off exit to Kenwood Road, left on Kenwood Road; Kenwood Shopping Center on right; (513) 984–2361
7030 Reading Road—Swifton Commons Shopping Center; (513) 351–5712

Hours: 10:00 A.M.–9:00 P.M., Monday–Saturday; noon–5:00 or 6:00 P.M., Sunday, varies by location
Credit Cards: American Express, Discover, Elder-Beerman, MasterCard, Visa

Personal Checks: Yes
Handicapped Accessible: Most locations
Food: Outlets located in shopping centers or business districts with fast food nearby
Bus Tours: Yes

Factory Direct
10737 Reading Road

Directions: Exit 14 off I–75; north on Reading Road to store on left side of street
Phone: (513) 733–0800
Hours: 9:30 A.M.–8:00 P.M., Monday–Friday; 9:00 A.M.–6:00 P.M., Saturday; noon–5:00 P.M., Sunday
Credit Cards: MasterCard, Visa, Ohio Golden Buckeye senior discount card
Personal Checks: Yes
Handicapped Accessible: Yes. Reserved parking in the front of store. Store is roomy with large doors and wide aisles.
Food: Restaurant (buffet-style) is across the street.
Bus Tours: Yes

Hit or Miss
three locations:
11392 Princeton Pike; (513) 671–3081
3960 E. Galbriath Road; (513) 793–3139
7500 Beechmont Mall; (513) 232–5440

Directions: Call ahead.
Hours: 10:00 A.M.–9:00 P.M., Monday–Saturday; noon–5:00 P.M., Sunday
Credit Cards: American Express, Discover, MasterCard, Visa
Personal Checks: Yes, from banks within a 60-mile radius
Handicapped Accessible: Yes
Food: Located in shopping centers or business districts with fast food nearby
Bus Tours: Yes

Men's Clothing Outlet, Inc.
202 Dixie Terminal Building South, 2nd floor
49 E. Fourth Street

Directions: In downtown Cincinnati at the southwest corner of Fourth and Walnut. Enter building at Fourth Street; go to rear of main lobby, walk up one flight on right side, and follow signs on second floor.
Phone: (513) 579–0033
Hours: 10:00 A.M.–5:00 P.M., Monday–Saturday
Credit Cards: MasterCard, Visa
Personal Checks: Yes, with proper identification
Handicapped Accessible: No; on second floor
Food: Restaurants and fast food in downtown area

Outlets Ltd. Mall
I–71 and King Mill Road

Directions: I–71 to exit 25 (King Mill Road), outlet on left-hand side
Phone: (513) 398–5532
Hours: 10:00 A.M.–9:00 P.M., Monday–Saturday; noon–6:00 P.M., Sunday
Outlets:
Aunt Mary's Yarns
Children's Outlet
Diamonds Unlimited
Dress Barn
Famous Footwear
Frontier Fruit & Nut Co.
Gold N Things
Hit or Miss
Jewelies
Linens 'n Things
Old Mill
The Paper Factory
Pottery and More
Prestige Fragrances & Cosmetics, Inc.
Shoe Manufacturers Outlets
Shoe Sensation
Socks Galore & More

Toy Liquidators
Van Heusen Factory Store
Welcome Home
Credit Cards: Most stores accept major credit cards.
Personal Checks: Most stores accept checks with two forms of proper identification.
Handicapped Accessible: Yes
Food: Fast food and restaurants at Exit 25
Bus Tours: Yes
Notes or Attractions: Across from King's Island Amusement Park

Polly Flinders
234 E. 8th Street

Directions: Downtown Cincinnati; call ahead.
Phone: (513) 621–3222
Hours: 9:30 A.M.–5:00 P.M., Monday–Saturday
Credit Cards: MasterCard, Visa
Personal Checks: Yes, with proper identification
Handicapped Accessible: No
Food: Restaurants and fast food in downtown area
Bus Tours: No
Notes or Attractions: Close to all Cincinnati museums and attractions

Shapely Outlet Mall
2430 E. Kemper Road

Directions: I–275 to Mosteller Road exit, left to Kemper, right to Shapely Outlet Mall
Phone: (513) 771–9828
Hours: 10:00 A.M.–9:00 P.M., Monday–Saturday; noon–5:00 P.M., Sunday
Outlets:
Annie's Son Shoes
Cotton Mill
Fashion Factory Outlet

Head Factory Outlet
Jewelies
Newport Menswear
Old Mill
Polly Flinders
Shapely Factory Outlet
Credit Cards: Stores honor most major credit cards.
Personal Checks: Most stores accept checks with proper identification.
Handicapped Accessible: Yes
Food: Cafe in mall
Bus Tours: Yes

CLEVELAND

Joseph & Feiss Company Outlet Store
2149 W. 53rd Street

Directions: I–90 to West 44th exit, right to Clark Avenue, right to West 53rd, and a right on Walworth to rear entrance of outlet
Phone: (216) 961–3907
Hours: 1:30–8:30 P.M., Wednesday and Friday; 4:30–8:30 P.M., Thursday; 10:00 A.M.–6:00 P.M., Saturday; 11:00 A.M.–5:00 P.M., Sunday
Additional Savings: Seasonal closeout sales June and December
Credit Cards: MasterCard, Visa
Personal Checks: Yes, with driver's license
Handicapped Accessible: Yes
Food: Fast food and restaurants within 3 miles
Bus Tours: Yes; call in advance.

COLUMBUS

Bike Nashbar Outlet Store
4733 Reed Road, Arlington Square Shopping Center

Directions: Route 315 to Henderson Road West. From Henderson, make a left onto Reed Road and into shopping center.
Phone: (614) 442–0202
Hours: 10:00 A.M.–8:00 P.M., Monday–Friday; 10:00 A.M.–6:00 P.M., Saturday; noon–4:00 P.M., Sunday in December and April to September
Additional Savings: Anniversary Sale, August; President's Day Sale, February; Spring Sale, March; TOSRV Ride Sale, April; Moonlight Madness Sale, July; Pre-Inventory Sale, September
Credit Cards: Discover, MasterCard, Visa
Personal Checks: Yes, with proper identification
Handicapped Accessible: Yes
Food: In and around shopping center
Bus Tours: Yes
Notes or Attractions: Bike-riding paths nearby; close to Columbus Zoo.

Brice Road Consumer Square
Brice and Tussing Roads

Directions: Take Brice Road exit south off I–70; at first light (Tussing Road) make a left.
Phone: No on-site phone
Hours: 10:00 A.M.–9:00 P.M., Monday–Saturday; noon–5:00 P.M., Sunday
Outlets:
Burlington Coat Factory Warehouse
The Clothes Store
Dress Barn
Drug Emporium
The Finish Line

Kids Mart
Old Mill Clearance Center
Silk Greenhouse
Sycamore
Credit Cards: Most stores accept major credit cards.
Personal Checks: Most stores accept checks with proper identification.
Handicapped Accessible: Yes
Food: Fast food and restaurants in center out-lot
Bus Tours: Yes

Burlington Coat Factory Warehouse
270 Graceland Boulevard

Directions: Take I–71 to Morse Road exit; west on Morse until intersection with High Street (Rte. 23). Turn right onto High. At first light, take left onto Graceland Boulevard, which takes you right into shopping center.
Phone: (614) 885–2628
Hours: 10:00 A.M.–9:00 P.M., Monday–Saturday; 11:00 A.M.–6:00 P.M., Sunday
Credit Cards: American Express, Discover, MasterCard, Visa
Personal Checks: Yes, with driver's license
Handicapped Accessible: Yes
Food: Fast food nearby
Bus Tours: Yes

The Clothes Store
five locations:
1198 Kenney Square Mall; (614) 459–0846
1010 Morse Road; (614) 888–5638
7608 NewMarket Center Way; (614) 766–6310
6448 Tussing Road; (614) 863–3017
93 Westerville Plaza; (614) 882–5370

Directions: Call ahead.
Hours: 10:00 A.M.–9:00 P.M., Monday–Saturday; noon–6:00 P.M., Sunday
Credit Cards: Discover, MasterCard, Visa
Personal Checks: Yes, with proper identification
Handicapped Accessible: Yes
Food: Fast food nearby
Bus Tours: Yes

Dress Barn
four locations:
W. Broad & Wilson Road; (614) 279–2935
7624 NewMarket Center Way; (614) 764–0557
5614 Cleveland Avenue; (614) 882–5533
6464 Tussing Road; (614) 863–0041

Directions: Call ahead.
Hours: 10:00 A.M.–9:00 P.M., Monday–Saturday; noon–5:00 P.M., Sunday
Credit Cards: American Express, Discover, MasterCard, Visa
Personal Checks: Yes, with proper identification
Handicapped Accessible: Yes
Food: Fast food nearby
Bus Tours: Yes

El-Bee Shoe Outlets
eight locations:
113 Graceland Boulevard; (614) 885–8332
7616 NewMarket Center Way; (614) 764–2469
1831 W. Henderson Road; (614) 457–8720
52 Westerville Square; (614) 882–4809
124 Wilson Road; (614) 272–0257
2711 Northland Plaza; (614) 891–4774
5803 Scarborough Mallway; (614) 868–5661

Directions: Call ahead.

Hours: 10:00 A.M.–9:00 P.M., Monday–Saturday; noon–5:00 P.M., Sunday
Credit Cards: American Express, Discover, Elder-Beerman, MasterCard, Visa
Personal Checks: Yes
Handicapped Accessible: Most outlets
Food: Outlets are located in shopping centers close to fast food and restaurants.
Bus Tours: Yes

Famous Footwear
seven locations:
859 Bethel Road; (614) 451–1115
4408 Crossroads Center; (614) 866–9857
NewMarket Center Way; (614) 766–6777
4121 W. Broad Street; (614) 274–0855
5840 Scarborough Mallway; (614) 863–0884
2703 Northland Plaza; (614) 794–2102
3764 E. Broad Street; (614) 231–0722

Directions: Call ahead.
Hours: 10:00 A.M.–9:00 P.M., Monday–Saturday; noon–5:00 P.M., Sunday
Additional Savings: Frequent in-store specials
Credit Cards: MasterCard, Visa
Personal Checks: Yes, with driver's license and phone numbers (work and home)
Handicapped Accessible: Yes
Food: Fast food usually nearby—stores located in shopping districts
Bus Tours: Yes

Frugal Fox Wallpaper Outlet
three locations:
60 E. Powell Road; (614) 847–9511
1735 Brice Road; (614) 755–9411
634 W. Schrock Road; (614) 898–6996

Directions: Call ahead.
Hours: 10:00 A.M.–8:00 P.M., Monday–Friday, 10:00 A.M.–6:00 P.M., Saturday; noon–5:00 P.M., Sunday
Credit Cards: American Express, MasterCard, Visa
Personal Checks: Yes
Handicapped Accessible: Powell Road, no; Brice Road, store interior accessible but no curb ramp outside; W. Schrock Road, yes
Food: Nearby
Bus Tours: Yes

Hit or Miss
five locations:
2025 W. Henderson Road; (614) 451–0628
4617 Morse Road; (614) 436–2946
3760 E. Broad Street; (614) 237–8090
4428 Hamilton Road; (614) 864–3967
NewMarket Center Way; (614) 766–6777

Directions: Call ahead.
Hours: 10:00 A.M.–9:00 P.M., Monday–Saturday; noon–5:00 P.M., Sunday
Additional Savings: Merchandise frequently marked down
Credit Cards: American Express, Discover, MasterCard, Visa
Personal Checks: Yes, from banks within 60-mile radius
Handicapped Accessible: Yes
Food: Fast food usually nearby—outlets located in shopping districts
Bus Tours: Yes

J. C. Penney Catalog Outlet Store
Brice Road

Directions: I–70 to Brice Road South. Turn right at first light, Scarborough Road, and go about 1 mile. Building is on left.
Phone: (614) 868–0250
Hours: 9:00 A.M.–9:00 P.M., Monday–Saturday; 10:00 A.M.–7:00 P.M., Sunday

Additional Savings: Weekly advertised sales plus seasonal clearance sales
Credit Cards: American Express, J. C. Penney, MasterCard, Visa
Personal Checks: Yes, with proper identification
Handicapped Accessible: Yes
Food: Snack bar in store, fast food and restaurants at Brice and Scarborough roads.
Bus Tours: Yes
Notes or Attractions: Close to all Columbus events and attractions

J. C. Penney Furniture Warehouse Outlet
Central Point Shopping Center, Harrisburg Pike

Directions: Take Sullivant Avenue/Mound Street exit off I–70. Make a right onto Mound Street. At second traffic light (Harrisburg Pike), make a left. Shopping center is directly on your right.
Phone: (614) 274–8409
Hours: 10:00 A.M.–8:00 P.M., Monday–Friday; 10:00 A.M.–6:00 P.M., Saturday; noon–5:00 P.M., Sunday
Credit Cards: American Express, J. C. Penney, MasterCard, Visa
Personal Checks: Yes, with proper identification
Handicapped Accessible: Yes
Food: In shopping center
Bus Tours: Yes
Notes or Attractions: Near Cooper Stadium and other Columbus attractions

Lazarus Final Clearance & Furniture Warehouse Outlet
141 S. High Street

Directions: Intersection of S. High and W. Town streets in center of Columbus. Final Clearance is at the Front Street level; Furniture Warehouse is on the sixth floor.
Phone: Final Clearance, (614) 463–3520; Warehouse Outlet, (614) 463–3521

Hours: 10:00 A.M.–9:00 P.M., Monday–Friday; 10:00 A.M.–6:00 P.M., Saturday; noon–6:00 P.M., Sunday
Credit Cards: Lazarus charge, MasterCard, Visa
Personal Checks: Yes; two identifications are required, one with a photograph.
Handicapped Accessible: Yes
Food: Fast food and restaurants in downtown area; links into City Center Mall

Madison's Grand Finale
Festival Place Shopping Center

Directions: South of Route 161 on Sawmill Road
Phone: (614) 764–1757
Hours: 10:00 A.M.–9:00 P.M., Monday–Saturday; noon–6:00 P.M., Sunday
Credit Cards: Discover, MasterCard, Visa
Personal Checks: Yes, with proper identification
Handicapped Accessible: Yes
Food: Restaurant in shopping center; fast food nearby
Bus Tours: Yes

NewMarket Mall
I–270 at Sawmill Road

Directions: Take exit 20 (Sawmill Road) off I–270 and head north; mall entrance is on your right.
Phone: (614) 766–6777
Hours: 10:00 A.M.–9:00 P.M., Monday–Saturday; noon–6:00 P.M., Sunday
Additional Savings: Seasonal sales the third weekend in January, the second weekend in March, the second weekend in July
Outlets:
Amy Stoudt
Beauty Fair USA
Casual Male Big and Tall

The Clothes Store
Dress Barn/Dress Barn Woman
Eagle Clothes
El-Bee Shoes
Famous Footwear
The Finish Line
Hit or Miss
Kitchen Place
Linens 'n Things
Old Mill
Paper Factory
Plumm's
S & K Famous Brands
Shoe Sensation
Credit Cards: All stores accept most major credit cards.
Personal Checks: Most stores require two forms of proper identification.
Handicapped Accessible: Yes
Food: Restaurant and fast food in mall
Bus Tours: Yes
Notes or Attractions: Near Columbus zoo and historic old Dublin; other Columbus attractions one-half hour away

Nu-Look Fashions Factory Outlet
5080 Sinclair Road

Directions: Take I–71 to Morse Road West exit; turn right onto Sinclair Road. Store is on your right.
Phone: (614) 885–4936
Hours: 10:00 A.M.–7:00 P.M., Monday–Friday; 10:00 A.M.–6:00 P.M., Saturday
Credit Cards: MasterCard, Visa
Personal Checks: Yes, with driver's license
Handicapped Accessible: One step into store, security guard or store personnel will provide assistance.
Food: Fast food and restaurants all along Morse Road
Bus Tours: Yes

Scarborough Mall
Brice and Scarborough Roads

Directions: I–70 to Brice Road South exit. Go right at first intersection (Scarborough Road). Mall is on your left.
Phone: (614) 863–0884
Hours: 10:00 A.M.–9:00 P.M., Monday–Saturday; noon–5:00 P.M., Sunday
Outlets:
Amy Stoudt
Beauty Fair USA
Bon Worth Factory Outlet
Book Warehouse
Eagle Clothes
Famous Footwear
Fashions 4 Kids
Ninth Street Bridal and Formal Outlet
Plumm's
Shoe Sensation
Watches-N-Stuff
Credit Cards: Most stores accept major credit cards.
Personal Checks: Most stores accept checks with two forms of proper identification.
Handicapped Accessible: Yes
Food: In mall
Bus Tours: Yes
Notes or Attractions: Near Brice Road Consumer Square shopping center and J. C. Penney Catalog Outlet; Super Saver Cinemas, with eight screens and $1.50 admission at all times, in mall.

Sears Outlet
4545 Fisher Road; (614) 272–3001

Directions: Call ahead.
Hours: 10:00 A.M.–9:00 P.M., Monday–Friday; 10:00 A.M.–6:00 P.M., Saturday; noon–5:00 P.M., Sunday
Credit Cards: Discover, Sears

Personal Checks: Yes, with proper identification
Handicapped Accessible: Yes
Food: Fast food nearby
Bus Tours: Yes

Silk Greenhouse
three locations:
Reed and Henderson Roads; (614) 442–3311
I–70 and Brice Road; (614) 759–9590
W. Broad and Wilson Road; (614) 351–1700

Directions: Call ahead.
Hours: 10:00 A.M.–9:00 P.M., Monday–Saturday; noon–5:00 P.M., Sunday
Credit Cards: MasterCard, Visa
Personal Checks: Yes, with driver's license
Handicapped Accessible: Yes
Food: Fast food nearby
Bus Tours: Yes

Sycamore
three locations:
Route 161 and Cleveland Avenue; (614) 891–9303
6472 Tussing Road; (614) 755–2216
Westerville Mall; (614) 898–7769

Directions: Call ahead.
Hours: 10:00 A.M.–9:00 P.M., Monday–Saturday; noon–5:00 P.M., Sunday
Credit Cards: MasterCard, Visa
Personal Checks: Yes, with driver's license
Handicapped Accessible: Yes
Food: Locations in shopping center with food nearby
Bus Tours: Yes

DAYTON

Book Warehouse
Corners at the Mall Shopping Center
231 Springboro Pike

Directions: Call ahead.
Phone: (513) 438–9119
Hours: 10:00 A.M.–9:00 P.M., Monday–Saturday; noon–5:00 P.M., Sunday
Credit Cards: Diners Club, Discover, MasterCard, Visa
Personal Checks: Yes
Handicapped Accessible: Yes, with handicapped parking in front of store
Food: Fast food and restaurants in front of shopping center
Bus Tours: Yes
Notes or Attractions: Air Force Museum, the oldest and largest military aviation museum in the world, located at Wright-Patterson Air Force Base, and self-guided Aviation Trail, connecting historic aviation sites, are both in Dayton.

El-Bee Shoe Outlet
five locations:
143 N. Main Street, southwest corner of Main and First streets in downtown Dayton; (513) 222–5784
Van Buren Shopping Center, 1328 Forrer Boulevard, corner of Forrer and Smithville Road; (513) 253–2737
Eastown Shopping Center, 3954 Linden Avenue, 1 block west of Woodman Drive; (513) 253–9091
Southtown Shopping Center, 2410 Miamisburg-Centerville Road, next to the Dayton Mall; (513) 433–3663
Northwest Plaza Shopping Center, 3207 Siebenthaler Avenue, adjacent to Elder-Beerman department store; (513) 274–1525

Hours: 10:00 A.M.–9:00 P.M., Monday–Saturday; noon–5:00 P.M., Sunday

Credit Cards: American Express, Discover, Elder-Beerman, MasterCard, Visa
Personal Checks: Yes
Handicapped Accessible: Partial
Food: In and near shopping center
Bus Tours: Yes

Hit or Miss
Salem Mall, 5200 Salem Avenue

Directions: Call ahead.
Phone: (513) 837–2817
Hours: 10:00 A.M.–9:00 P.M., Monday–Saturday; noon–5:00 P.M., Sunday
Additional Savings: Merchandise frequently marked down
Credit Cards: American Express, Discover, MasterCard, Visa
Personal Checks: Yes, from banks within a 60-mile radius
Handicapped Accessible: Yes
Food: Available in and near shopping center
Bus Tours: Yes
Notes or Attractions: Air Force Museum, the oldest and largest military aviation museum in the world, located at Wright-Patterson Air Force Base, and self-guided Aviation Trail, connecting historic aviation sites, are both in Dayton.

Midwest Glass & China Outlet
6425 N. Dixie Drive

Directions: From I–75, take exit 58 West (Needmore Road) ½ mile to N. Dixie Drive; outlet is ½-mile north on west side of N. Dixie Drive.
Phone: (513) 890–1009
Hours: 10:00 A.M.–6:00 P.M., Monday–Saturday; noon–4:00 P.M., Sunday (winter only)
Credit Cards: MasterCard, Visa
Personal Checks: Yes, with proper identification
Handicapped Accessible: Yes, with entrance ramp, wide aisles, and first-floor restroom

Food: Restaurant next door
Bus Tours: Yes
Notes or Attractions: Air Force Museum, the oldest and largest military aviation museum in the world, located at Wright-Patterson Air Force Base, and self-guided Aviation Trail, connecting historic aviation sites, are both in Dayton.

LANCASTER

Footsaver Shoes
252 Quarry Road

Directions: Four and one half miles east of Route 33 off State Route 22
Phone: (614) 687–3322
Hours: 9:00 A.M.–5:00 P.M., Monday–Friday; 10:00 A.M.–4:00 P.M., Saturday
Additional Savings: Seasonal sales every three to four months
Credit Cards: MasterCard, Visa
Personal Checks: Yes, with driver's license or photo identification
Handicapped Accessible: Yes
Food: Fast food, diners, and restaurants along routes 22 and 33
Bus Tours: Yes
Notes or Attractions: Close to Wahkeena and Schallenbarger nature preserves; more than ten covered bridges within a 15-mile radius

Kitchen Collection Factory Outlet Store
621 N. Memorial Drive

Directions: On Route 33 at the intersection of 6th Avenue and Memorial Drive
Phone: (614) 687–1750
Hours: 10:00 A.M.–9:00 P.M., Monday–Saturday; noon–6:00 P.M., Sunday

Additional Savings: Monthly sales
Credit Cards: MasterCard, Visa
Personal Checks: Yes, with driver's license or photo identification
Handicapped Accessible: Yes
Food: Along Route 33
Bus Tours: Yes, 10 percent discount to bus groups

MAPLE HEIGHTS

American Commodore Tuxedo
5147 Warrensville Center Road

Directions: At Warrensville Center between Libby Road and Emery Road
Phone: (216) 663–6688
Hours: 10:00 A.M.–5:00 P.M., Saturday
Credit Cards: American Express, Diners Club, Discover, MasterCard, Visa
Personal Checks: Yes, with an Ohio driver's license and major credit card; no out-of-state checks
Handicapped Accessible: There are twelve stairs.
Food: Available nearby
Bus Tours: Yes
Notes or Attractions: Near Randall Park Mall

MARIETTA

Middleton Doll Factory Outlet
268 Front Street

Directions: Take I–77 to Marietta exit, which turns into Pike and then runs into Green Street; make right onto Front. Outlet is near Ohio River and post office.

Phone: (614) 374–3655
Hours: 10:00 A.M.–5:00 P.M., Monday–Saturday
Credit Cards: MasterCard, Visa
Personal Checks: Yes, with proper identification
Handicapped Accessible: Yes
Food: Nearby
Bus Tours: Yes
Notes or Attractions: Near Campus Martius Museum, Ohio River Museum, and Ohio River

MASSILLON

Ekco Housewares Outlet Store
359 State Avenue, NW

Directions: Take Route 77 to 172 West (Lincoln Way); continue with a right onto Erie and a left on Cherry. Cross over Route 21 and a bridge; turn right immediately after bridge onto Third Street. Follow signs for remainder of directions.
Phone: (216) 832–5026
Hours: 10:30 A.M.–2:00 P.M., Tuesday and Thursday
Credit Cards: No
Personal Checks: Yes, with driver's license
Handicapped Accessible: No
Food: Fast food within 1 mile
Bus Tours: No
Notes or Attractions: Small parking lot for customers

El-Bee Shoe Outlet
2476 Lincoln Way East

Directions: Take Route 77 to 250 West, then 21 North; go right at Lincoln Way 4 miles to Pak Park Center
Phone: (216) 493–8195

Hours: 10:00 A.M.–9:00 P.M., Monday–Saturday; noon–5:00 P.M., Sunday
Credit Cards: American Express, Discover, Elder-Beerman, MasterCard, Visa
Personal Checks: Yes
Handicapped Accessible: Partial
Food: Fast food nearby
Bus Tours: Yes

MIDDLEBURG HEIGHTS

Richmond Brothers Outlet Store
Southland Center
W. 130th and Pearl Road

Directions: Take I–71 to Route 42 North (Pearl Road). Center is on your right.
Phone: (216) 843–6840
Hours: 10:00 A.M.–9:00 P.M., Monday–Saturday
Credit Cards: American Express, Discover, MasterCard, Visa
Personal Checks: Yes, with two proper identifications
Handicapped Accessible: Yes
Food: Restaurant in center, fast food nearby
Bus Tours: Yes

MILAN

Lake Erie Factory Outlet
11001 U.S. Route 250N

Directions: On U.S. 250, ½ mile north of exit 7 of the Ohio Turnpike (I–80/90) and 5 miles south of Route 2
Phone: (800) 344–5221

Hours: January through March—10:00 A.M.–6:00 P.M., Monday–Wednesday; 10:00 A.M.–9:00 P.M., Thursday–Saturday; noon–6:00 P.M., Sunday; April through December—10:00 A.M.–9:00 P.M., Monday–Saturday; 10:00 A.M.–6:00 P.M., Sunday

Outlets:

Aileen
American Tourister
Banister Shoes
Bass Shoes
China Plus
Corning/Revere
Factory Linens
Fanny Farmer
Farberware
Gitano
Hanes
harvé benard
Hilda of Iceland
Jonathan Logan
Just Pants
Kelli's
Kitchen Collection
Leather Loft
Manhattan
Mikasa
Nilani
No Nonsense
Old Mill
Paper Factory
Prestige Fragrance
The Ribbon Outlet
Ruff Hewn
S & K Famous Brands
Socks Galore
Sweatshirt Company
Toy Liquidators
Van Heusen Outlet Store
Wallet Works
Welcome Home
Wemco

Westport Ltd.
What A Deal
Credit Cards: Most major credit cards are accepted.
Personal Checks: Most stores accept personal checks with two forms of proper identification.
Handicapped Accessible: Yes
Food: Food court in mall
Bus Tours: Yes
Notes or Attractions: Reserved parking for buses, RVs, and campers; located near Lake Erie beaches and resorts, wineries, and Cedar Point Amusement Park

MONROE

Fostoria Factory Outlet
1009 Lebanon Street

Directions: Take I–71 to Lebanon exit (Route 63); turn right and continue until Route 63 intersects with I–75.
Phone: (513) 539–9632
Hours: 9:00 A.M.–5:00 P.M., Monday–Sunday
Credit Cards: MasterCard, Visa
Personal Checks: Yes, with driver's license
Handicapped Accessible: Yes
Food: Next door
Bus Tours: Yes

NELSONVILLE

Brooks Boot & Shoe Factory Outlet
State Road 33

Directions: Brick factory building located at the intersection of Route 33 and Hocking Street; factory outlet in back

Phone: (614) 753–3130
Hours: 9:00 A.M.–7:00 P.M., Monday–Saturday; 11:30 A.M.–5:30 P.M., Sunday
Credit Cards: Discover, MasterCard, Visa
Personal Checks: Yes, with driver's license
Handicapped Accessible: On notification, personnel will assist in bringing customer through factory.
Food: Fast food and restaurants along Route 33
Bus Tours: Yes
Notes or Attractions: Near Hocking Valley Scenic Railroad

NILES

B & J Sales
Niles Park Plaza

Directions: Niles Park Plaza is located on Route 422 in Niles.
Phone: (216) 652–2729
Hours: 10:00 A.M.–6:00 P.M., Monday–Saturday
Additional Savings: Specials run prior to major gift-giving holidays
Credit Cards: Discover, MasterCard, Visa
Personal Checks: Yes, with proper identification
Handicapped Accessible: Yes
Food: Available next door
Bus Tours: Yes

El-Bee Shoe Outlet
945 Great East Plaza

Directions: From I–80, take Route 422 north 6 miles.
Phone: (216) 652–0433
Hours: 10:00 A.M.–9:00 P.M., Monday–Saturday; noon–5:00 P.M., Sunday
Credit Cards: American Express, Discover, Elder-Beerman, MasterCard, Visa

Phone: (216) 562–2000 or (800) 837–2001
Hours: 10:00 A.M.–6:00 P.M., Monday–Wednesday; 10:00 A.M.–9:00 P.M., Thursday–Saturday; 10:00 A.M.–5:00 P.M., Sunday
Outlets:
Aileen
American Tourister
Banister Shoes
Bass Shoes
Campus Factory Outlet
Cape Isle Knitters
Carlson's Christmas Collection
Carter's Childrenswear
Corning/Revere Ware
Crazy Horse
Gitano
Hanes Activewear
harvé benard
The Housewares Store
Jonathan Logan Outlet
Jones New York Factory Store
Leather Loft Stores
L'eggs/Hanes/Bali
Manhattan Factory Outlet
The Paper Factory
Prestige Fragrance & Cosmetics, Inc.
The Ribbon Outlet
Salem China
Sequels Book Outlet
Sports Wearhouse
Van Heusen Factory Outlet
The Wallet Works
Wayside Workshop
Welcome Home
Credit Cards: Most stores accept all major credit cards.
Personal Checks: Most stores accept personal checks.
Handicapped Accessible: Yes
Food: Restaurant and snack shops on premises
Bus Tours: Yes, coupon brochure featuring additional savings for groups; bus driver and escort receive a "$5.00 coin" redeemable at stores or eateries

f downtown Cleveland, three exits
ional Airport off I–480

lay–Saturday; noon–5:00 P.M., Sun-

a *South*
eri-Tux
as Shoes
ntry Shop

most major credit cards.
ccept checks with proper identifica-

t food and snack establishments and

nt to airport. The Ambassador Center
s stroller and wheelchair rental, pack-
s, coat and package checks, fax and

PORT CLINTON

USCO Factory Outlet
Route 2, Erie Industrial Park

Directions: Call ahead.
Phone: (419) 635–2000
Hours: 10:00 A.M.–5:00 P.M., Monday–Friday; 9:00 A.M.–5:00 P.M., Saturday
Credit Cards: MasterCard, Visa
Personal Checks: Yes, with proper identification
Handicapped Accessible: Yes
Bus Tours: Yes

ST. MARYS

Cotton Mill Store
119 E. High Street

Directions: From I–75, take Route 33 west to Route 66 until St. Marys exit; make a right onto High Street, then a left into store.
Phone: (419) 394–3064
Hours: 9:30 A.M.–8:00 P.M., Monday; 9:30 A.M.–5:00 P.M., Tuesday–Thursday and Saturday; 9:30 A.M.–9:00 P.M., Friday; noon–5:00 P.M., Sunday
Additional Savings: Holiday clearance first two weeks in January, spring clearance for two weeks from first Thursday in March, summer clearance for two weeks from first Thursday in August
Credit Cards: Discover, MasterCard, Visa
Personal Checks: Yes, with name embossed on check, driver's license, and major credit card
Handicapped Accessible: Yes, with ramp and railing
Food: In downtown St. Marys (several minutes' walk away)
Bus Tours: Yes
Notes or Attractions: Near St. Marys Lake and Erie Canal

TIPP CITY

Trophy Nut Store
320 N. Second Street

Directions: From I–75, take exit 68 (State Route 571 East); cross railroad tracks and go to third traffic light after tracks (Second Street); turn left to plant and store.
Phone: (513) 667–8478
Hours: 9:00 A.M.–5:00 P.M., Monday–Friday; 9:00 A.M.–2:00 P.M., Saturday
Additional Savings: During fall and Christmas seasons
Credit Cards: Most major credit cards
Personal Checks: Yes
Handicapped Accessible: Call ahead; they will bring you through back door to avoid steps
Food: Within 3 blocks
Bus Tours: Yes

TOLEDO

El-Bee Shoe Outlet
two locations:
Northtowne Square Mall, 343 New Towne Square Drive—I–75 to Route 184 (Alexis) West; (419) 476–4987
Miracle Mile Shopping Center, 4925 Jackman Road—I–75 to Route 184 (Alexis) West until Jackman Road; left on Jackman; (419) 472–5808

Hours: 10:00 A.M.–9:00 P.M., Monday–Saturday; noon–5:00 P.M., Sunday
Credit Cards: American Express, Discover, Elder-Beerman, MasterCard, Visa
Personal Checks: Yes
Handicapped Accessible: Partial

Food: In or near shopping center
Bus Tours: Yes

Libbey Glass Factory Outlet Store
1205 Buckeye Street

Directions: From I–280, turn right at Manhattan exit; then make a quick left onto Buckeye Street, adjacent to the glass factory.
Phone: (419) 727–2374
Hours: 9:30 A.M.–5:30 P.M., Monday–Saturday; noon–5:00 P.M., Sunday, June–December
Credit Cards: MasterCard, Visa
Personal Checks: Yes, with proper identification
Handicapped Accessible: Yes
Food: Within a mile, with Tony Packo's world-famous Hungarian hot dogs an option
Bus Tours: Yes; $5.00 gift certificate given to driver and tour guide
Notes or Attractions: Contact Toledo Convention & Visitors Bureau at (800) 243–4667

YOUNGSTOWN

B & J Sales
398 E. Rayen Avenue

Directions: Take Route 422 to E. Rayen Avenue and proceed to corner of E. Rayen and Andrews avenues.
Phone: (216) 747–3341
Hours: 10:00 A.M.–6:00 P.M., Monday–Saturday
Additional Savings: Specials run prior to major gift-giving holidays
Credit Cards: Discover, MasterCard, Visa
Personal Checks: Yes, with proper identification
Handicapped Accessible: Yes
Notes or Attractions: Near Youngstown State University

Bike Nashbar Outlet Store
4111 Simon Road

Directions: Take exit 9A (Route 625/Midlothian Boulevard) off Route 680. From Midlothian Boulevard, go left onto Simon Road for 1 block; building is on the left.
Phone: (216) 782–2244
Hours: 10:00 A.M.–8:00 P.M., Monday–Friday; 10:00 A.M.–6:00 P.M., Saturday; noon–4:00 P.M., Sunday, December and April–September
Credit Cards: Discover, MasterCard, Visa
Personal Checks: Yes, with proper identification
Handicapped Accessible: Yes
Bus Tours: Yes

El-Bee Shoe Outlet
Great Boardmen Plaza
277 Boardmen Plaza/Canfield Road

Directions: From Route 11, go 3 miles east on Route 224
Phone: (216) 652–0433
Hours: 10:00 A.M.–9:00 P.M., Monday–Saturday; noon–5:00 P.M., Sunday
Credit Cards: American Express, Discover, Elder-Beerman, MasterCard, Visa
Personal Checks: Yes
Handicapped Accessible: Partial
Food: In or near shopping center
Bus Tours: Yes

Remember that outlets accepting personal checks require at least two forms of proper identification, usually a driver's license and a major credit card.

WISCONSIN

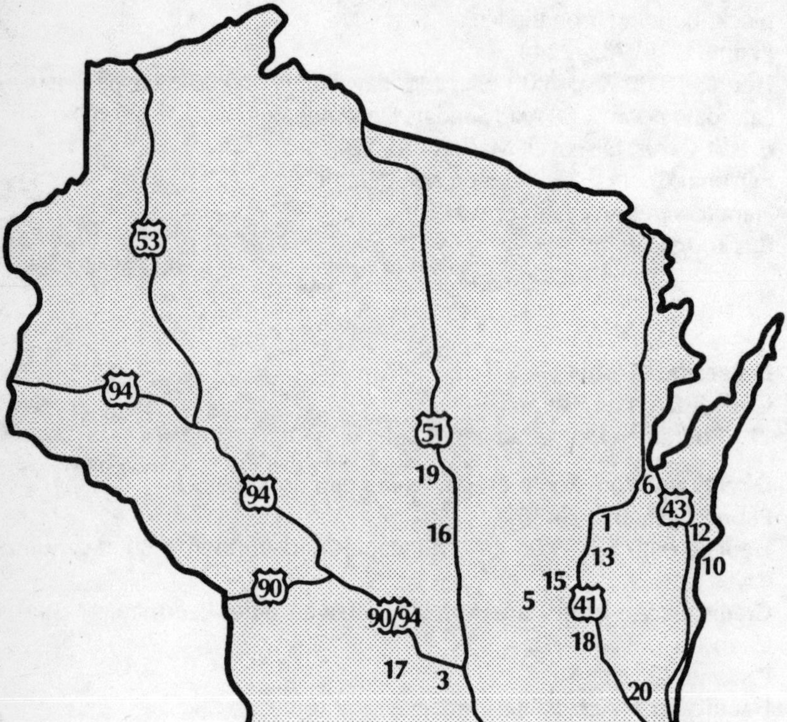

53
94
94
51
19
16
90
90/94
17
3
2
9
14
7
4
6
43
1
12
13
10
15
41
5
18
20
94
11
94
8

WISCONSIN

Numbers to the left of entries in this legend correspond to the numbers on the accompanying map. The number to the right of each city's or town's name is the page number on which that municipality's outlets first appear.

APPLETON

Benetton Factory Store
Fox River Mall
4301 W. Wisconsin Avenue

Directions: From Highway 41, exit to Highway 10.
Phone: (414) 734–0773
Hours: 10:00 A.M.–9:00 P.M., Monday–Friday; 10:00 A.M.–6:00 P.M., Saturday; 11:00 A.M.–5:00 P.M., Sunday
Additional Savings: November–January and July
Credit Cards: American Express, MasterCard, Visa
Personal Checks: Yes, with proper identification
Handicapped Accessible: Yes
Food: Food court in mall
Bus Tours: Yes
Notes or Attractions: Fifteen miles from EAA Air Adventure Museum in Oshkosh, 35 miles from Green Bay Packer Hall of Fame

ARENA

Farmer's Pride Cheese, Inc.
Box 127, Highway 14

Directions: Thirty miles west of Madison and 8 miles east of Spring Green on Highway 14
Phone: (608) 753–2501
Hours: 8:30 A.M.–7:00 P.M., daily
Credit Cards: Most major credit cards
Personal Checks: Yes, with driver's license
Handicapped Accessible: Yes
Food: Available at store
Bus Tours: Yes
Notes or Attractions: Observation window so that visitors can view the manufacturing process

BARABOO

Flambeau Outlet Store
611 Hitchcock Street

Directions: Corner of South Bend and Hitchcock (also known as City #12)
Phone: (608) 356–3602
Hours: 10:00 A.M.–5:00 P.M., Tuesday–Saturday
Credit Cards: No
Personal Checks: Yes, with proper identification
Handicapped Accessible: Yes
Food: Restaurants within several blocks

BELOIT

Freeman Outlet Mall
5 Freeman Lane

Directions: In Beloit Industrial Park, take exit 185A from I–90.
Phone: (608) 364–1334
Hours: 9:30 A.M.–9:00 P.M., Monday–Friday; 9:30 A.M.–6:00 P.M., Saturday; 10:30 A.M.–6:00 P.M., Sunday
Outlets:
Aileen
Banister Shoes
Fieldcrest Cannon
L'eggs/Hanes/Bali
Van Heusen Factory Store
Credit Cards: Most stores accept major credit cards.
Personal Checks: Most stores accept checks with two forms of proper identification.
Handicapped Accessible: Yes
Food: Snack shop in mall
Bus Tours: Yes
Notes or Attractions: Ninety minutes south of Wisconsin Dells, on the route to Devil's Head ski area

BERLIN

Midwestern Sports Togs/Berlin Glove Company
150 W. Franklin

Directions: In downtown Berlin, 20 miles west of Oshkosh on Route 116 at intersection of Route 49
Phone: (414) 361–2555
Hours: 8:00 A.M.–5:00 P.M., Monday–Friday, 8:00 A.M.–noon, Saturday; Thanksgiving through Christmas—10:00 A.M.–3:00 P.M., Sunday
Additional Savings: Fur and leather day sale during last weekend in August
Credit Cards: MasterCard, Visa
Personal Checks: No out-of-state checks
Handicapped Accessible: Yes
Food: Nearby downtown diners
Bus Tours: Yes
Notes or Attractions: Berlin is the fur and leather capitol of Wisconsin.

GREEN BAY

Herrschner's Crafts, Inc.
2977 Allied Drive

Directions: Highway 41 at Oneida Street exit, in the Chalet Complex
Phone: (414) 337–6654
Hours: 10:00 A.M.–5:00 P.M., Monday–Saturday; 11:00 A.M.–4:00 P.M., Sunday
Credit Cards: American Express, MasterCard, Visa
Personal Checks: No
Handicapped Accessible: Yes
Food: Available next door
Bus Tours: Yes
Notes or Attractions: Green Bay Packer Hall of Fame 1½ miles away

JANESVILLE

Monterey Mills Outlet Store
1725 E. Delavan Drive

Directions: From I–90, take Highway 11 West exit. Travel through town, make a left at Main Street, continue for a mile, and make a left onto Delavan. Outlet is a mile down the road on the left.
Phone: (608) 754–8309, (800) 438–6387
Hours: 8:00 A.M.–4:30 P.M., Monday–Friday; 8:00 A.M.–noon, Saturday
Credit Cards: MasterCard, Visa
Personal Checks: Yes, with driver's license and phone number noted on check
Handicapped Accessible: One step up from ground level
Food: Restaurants 2 to 3 miles from outlet
Bus Tours: Yes; must notify first
Notes or Attractions: Near General Motors plant and historic Tallman House

KENOSHA

Factory Outlet Center
7700 120th Avenue

Directions: From I–94 take exit 344 West (Kenosha/Lake Geneva or Route 50). Outlet center on left
Phone: (414) 857–7961
Hours: January through June—9:30 A.M.–9:00 P.M., Monday–Friday; 9:30 A.M.–6:00 P.M., Saturday; 11:00 A.M.–5:00 P.M., Sunday; July through December—9:30 A.M.–9:00 P.M., Monday–Friday; 9:30 A.M.–8:00 P.M., Saturday; 10:00 A.M.–6:00 P.M., Sunday
Outlets:
Aileen
Ambrosia Chocolate & Cocoa
American Tourister

Helly-Hansen
Hit or Miss
Home Decor Outlet
Houseware Outlet Store
Izod/Ship 'n Shore/Monet
Jonathan Logan Outlet
Julie's Jewelry
Just My Size
Kids Ca'pers
Knits by K.T.
LaCrosse Footware
L.A. Lifestyles
Lamp and Shade Outlet
L'eggs/Hanes/Bali
Lehmann's Danish Bakery and Kringle Outlet
Little Red Shoe House
Loomcraft Home Decorating Fabrics
Manhattan Factory Store
Maternity Warehouse
Mid American Shoes
Mill City Outlet
Mitchell Leather Shop
Multiples
Munsingwear
Newport for Men
New Visions
The Paint and Wallpaper Factory Outlet
Paper Factory
Perfume Boutique
Rainbow Fashions
Regal Ware Outlet
The Ribbon Outlet
S & K Famous Brands
70% Off
Shapes Activewear
Socks Galore and More
Sweats, Etc.
Top of the Line Cosmetics
totes
Toy King

Van Heusen Factory Store
Wallet Works
Welcome Home
The West Bend Company Store
Whitewater Gloves
Winona Knits
World Bazaar
Credit Cards: Most stores accept American Express, Discover, MasterCard, Visa
Personal Checks: Most stores accept checks with two forms of proper identification.
Handicapped Accessible: Yes
Food: Food court with more than ten food places to please everyone's tastes
Bus Tours: Yes

Lakeside Marketplace Outlet Center
11211 120th Avenue

Directions: I–94 to exit 347; 3 miles from Highway 50
Phone: (414) 857–2101
Hours: 9:00 A.M.–9:00 P.M., Monday–Saturday; 11:00 A.M.–7:00 P.M., Sunday
Outlets:
Adolfo II
American Tourister
Anne Klein
Argenti
Bass Shoe
Benetton
Brass Factory
Calvin Klein
Cambridge Dry Goods
Capezio
Crystal Works
E. J. Plum
European Collections/Oleg Cassini
Evan Picone

Fanny Farmer
Fenn Wright & Mason
The Genuine Article
Gilligan O'Malley
Gitano
harvé benard
Henson Lingerie Factory Store
I.B. Diffusions
J. Crew Factory Store
J. G. Hook Co.
J.H. Collectibles
Jindo Furs
J. Knitwear
Jones NY Factory Store
Jordache
Just Kids Outlet
Kenneth Cole Shoes
Kitchen Collection
Leather Loft
Liz Claiborne
Maidenform
Prestige Fragrance & Cosmetics
Royal Robbins
Sassafras
Tanner Factory Outlet
That's Our Bag
Toys Unlimited
Van Heusen
The Wool Shed

Credit Cards: Most stores honor most major credit cards.

Personal Checks: Most stores accept checks with proper identification.

Handicapped Accessible: Yes

Food: Restaurant in mall plus vending machines in lounge

Bus Tours: Yes

Notes or Attractions: Near Lake Michigan approximately 47 miles from Chicago and 35 miles from Milwaukee

MADISON

Burlington Coat Factory Warehouse
1810 West Beltline Highway

Directions: Todd Drive exit left off the Beltline
Phone: (608) 257–6505
Hours: 10:00 A.M.–9:00 P.M., Monday–Saturday; 11:00 A.M.–6:00 P.M., Sunday
Additional Savings: Ladies' coat sale in January
Credit Cards: All major credit cards plus Burlington Coat Factory Warehouse credit card
Personal Checks: Yes, with proper identification and major credit card
Handicapped Accessible: Yes
Food: Next door and within a 3-block radius
Bus Tours: Yes
Notes or Attractions: Near Capitol and Coliseum

Lands' End Not Quite Perfect Store
411 S. State Street

Directions: Near Lake Mendota, on State Street between West Gilman and West Gorham close to capitol
Phone: (608) 257–4999
Hours: 10:00 A.M.–8:00 P.M., Monday and Thursday; 10:00 A.M.–6:00 P.M., Tuesday, Wednesday, Friday, and Saturday; 11:00 A.M.–5:00 P.M., Sunday.
Credit Cards: American Express, MasterCard, Visa
Personal Checks: Yes, with proper identification
Handicapped Accessible: Yes, but aisles narrow; will move racks to accommodate wheelchairs
Food: Several restaurants within 2 blocks
Bus Tours: Yes

Lands' End Outlet
Westland Plaza
6743 Odana Road

Directions: From West Beltline Highway, which is Route 12/14, go to Gammon Road exit and turn right. Continue to Odana Road and make a right turn; shopping center is on the right.
Phone: (608) 833–3343
Hours: 9:00 A.M.–9:00 P.M., Monday–Friday; 9:00 A.M.–6:00 P.M., Saturday; 11:00 A.M.–5:00 P.M., Sunday
Credit Cards: American Express, MasterCard, Visa
Personal Checks: Yes, with proper identification
Handicapped Accessible: Yes
Food: In or near shopping center
Bus Tours: Yes

MANITOWOC

Schuette Factory Outlet
814 Jay Street

Directions: On Jay Street between South Eighth and South Ninth
Phone: (414) 684–5521 ext. 25; (800) 558–7740 ext. 2777
Hours: 9:00 A.M.–8:00 P.M., Monday and Friday; 9:00 A.M.–5:00 P.M., Tuesday–Thursday; 9:00 A.M.–4:00 P.M., Saturday
Additional Savings: Special sales in April and October; Dollar Days monthly
Credit Cards: MasterCard, Visa
Personal Checks: Yes, driver's license and proper identification are needed with out-of-state checks.
Handicapped Accessible: Yes
Food: Restaurants within walking distance
Bus Tours: Yes

MILWAUKEE

Burlington Coat Factory Warehouse
two locations:
College Avenue and 13th Street, College Avenue exit off I–94; (414) 764–2474
Mill Road Shopping Center, N. 76th Street and Mill Road; (414) 358–0500

Hours: 10:00 A.M.–9:00 P.M., Monday–Saturday; 11:00 A.M.–6:00 P.M., Sunday
Additional Savings: Ladies' coat sale in January
Credit Cards: All major credit cards plus Burlington Coat Factory Warehouse credit card
Personal Checks: Yes, with proper identification and major credit card
Handicapped Accessible: Check with each store.
Food: In or near shopping area
Bus Tours: Yes

Everitt Knitting Co. Outlet Store
234 W. Florida Street

Directions: South of downtown area off S. Second Street
Phone: (414) 276–4647
Hours: 10:00 A.M.–4:00 P.M., Monday–Friday
Credit Cards: No
Personal Checks: Yes, but no out-of-state checks
Handicapped Accessible: No
Food: Two miles from downtown restaurant area
Bus Tours: Yes
Notes or Attractions: Bring cash; outlet does not accept credit cards or out-of-state-checks.

Lands' End Combo Store
6780 Brown Deer Road

Directions: From Route 181, which is N. 76th Street, go to West

Brown Deer Road. Turn east. Store is on the left, across the street from 68th Street.
Phone: (414) 362–6940
Hours: Variable; call ahead.
Credit Cards: American Express, MasterCard, Visa
Personal Checks: Yes, with proper identification
Handicapped Accessible: Yes
Food: Four blocks from restaurants in North Ridge shopping area and mall.
Bus Tours: Yes

Purdy Products, Inc./Milwaukee Soap Company
two locations:
1526 N. 31st Street (factory); Expressway to 35th Street exit, north on 35th to Uliet, east on Uliet to 31st Street going north 2 blocks; (414) 344–5300
5260 S. 27th Street (store); Expressway to 27th Street exit South, store on east side of street next to Nevada Bob's; (414) 282–7880

Hours: Factory—8:00 A.M.–4:00 P.M., Monday–Friday; Store—9:00 A.M.–5:00 P.M., Monday–Thursday; 9:00 A.M.–6:00 P.M., Friday; 9:00 A.M.–5:00 P.M., Saturday
Credit Cards: Most major credit cards
Personal Checks: Yes, local only
Handicapped Accessible: Limited; call ahead
Food: Nearby at both locations
Bus Tours: Yes, with notice

MISHICOT

Andercraft Woods
Route 1, Box 91

Directions: Take Highway 147 to Mishicot and go east on Church Street to Andercraft, on south side of street.

Phone: (414) 755–4014
Hours: 8:00 A.M.–4:30 P.M., Monday–Friday; 9:00 A.M.–4:00 P.M., Saturday; 1:00–4:00 P.M., Sunday
Credit Cards: American Express, MasterCard, Visa
Personal Checks: Yes
Handicapped Accessible: Yes
Food: Half mile from factory
Bus Tours: Yes

NEENAH

Jersild Factory Store
318 First Street

Directions: One block north of Theda Clark Hospital
Phone: (414) 725–6912
Hours: 9:00 A.M.–5:00 P.M., Monday–Friday; 9:00 A.M.–4:00 P.M., Saturday
Credit Cards: No
Personal Checks: No
Handicapped Accessible: No
Food: Within 4 block radius
Bus Tours: Yes
Notes or Attractions: Factory tours, lasting thirty to forty minutes, are available for groups of ten or more; reservations are necessary.

NEW GLARUS

Swiss Miss Textile Mart
Highway 69 South at Eleventh Avenue

Directions: One-half hour south of Madison on Highway 69
Phone: No phone on site

Hours: 9:00 A.M.–5:00 P.M., Monday–Saturday; noon–4:00 P.M., Sunday
Additional Savings: Annual sale third Wednesday through Sunday in July
Credit Cards: No
Personal Checks: Yes, with proper identification
Handicapped Accessible: Yes
Food: Homemade foods available in bowling alley next door
Bus Tours: Yes
Notes or Attractions: Free factory tours Monday through Friday from 8:00 A.M. to 4:00 P.M.

OSHKOSH

Carolina Designs Factory Outlet
627 Bay Shore Drive

Directions: Five blocks off Main Street on Lake Winnebago
Phone: (414) 231–9620
Hours: 10:00 A.M.–5:00 P.M., Monday–Saturday
Additional Savings: Summer sale last week in July through third week in August, Christmas Sale day after Thanksgiving to December 24
Credit Cards: American Express, Discover, MasterCard, Visa
Personal Checks: Yes, with proper identification
Handicapped Accessible: Yes
Food: Restaurants within several blocks
Bus Tours: Yes
Notes or Attractions: On Lake Winnebago and near EAA Air Adventure Museum

Manufacturers Marketplace
U.S. 41 and Highway 44

Directions: On U.S. 41 south of Highway 44
Phone: (616) 728–5170

Hours: 10:00 A.M.–9:00 P.M., Monday–Saturday; 11:00 A.M.–7:00 P.M., Sunday

Outlets:

Aileen
American Tourister
Aunt Mary's Yarns
Banister
Barbizon
Bass Shoes
Book Warehouse
Bugle Boy
Cape Isle Knitters
Clothesworks
Dansk
Farah
Fieldcrest Cannon
Fragrance World
Gitano
harvé benard
J.H. Collectibles
Johnston Fashions for Children
Jordache
KidsPort USA
Kitchen Collection
Leather Loft
L'eggs/Hanes/Bali
Little Red Shoe House
Mackintosh of New England
Manhattan
Maus Import Jewelry
Newport Sportswear
Nickels Company Store
Old Mill
OshKosh B'Gosh
Paper Factory
The Ribbon Outlet
Royal Doulton
Russell
Socks Galore
Specials—Exclusively Levi Strauss & Co.

Sports Factory
Stone Mountain Handbags
The Sweatshirt Company
Tanner Factory Store
Tool Warehouse
Toy Liquidators
Van Heusen
Welcome Home
Westport, Ltd.
Winona Knits
Credit Cards: Most stores accept major credit cards.
Personal Checks: Most stores accept checks with proper identification.
Handicapped Accessible: Yes
Food: Food court within mall
Bus Tours: Yes
Notes or Attractions: EAA Air Adventure Museum across the highway

PLOVER

Manufacturers Direct Mall & Outlet Center
101–17 Plover Road

Directions: Take exit 153 onto County Highway B from U.S. Highway 51.
Phone: (715) 341–7980
Hours: 9:30 A.M.–9:00 P.M., Monday–Friday; 9:30 A.M.–6:00 P.M., Saturday; 10:00 A.M.–6:00 P.M., Sunday
Outlets:
Aileen
Aunt Mary's Yarns
Bargain Fabrics
Clothes Connection
Cookie Jar Outlet
Creative Touch
The Discounter
The Genuine Article

House of Large Sizes
Houseware Outlet Store
K & M Bed and Bath
Little Red Shoe House
Old Mill Ladies Sportswear Factory Outlet
Paper Factory
Rainbow Sunglasses
Rainbow Times
Rybicki's Cheese Store
70% Off
Shoe Factory Clearance Center
Van Heusen Factory Store
Winona Knits
Credit Cards: Most merchants accept major cards.
Personal Checks: Most stores accept checks with proper identification.
Handicapped Accessible: Yes
Food: Restaurant, cocktail bar, and snack vendors are in the mall.
Bus Tours: Yes
Notes or Attractions: Adjacent to Rainbow Falls Amusement Park, with rides, water sports, and mini golf; bank branch in mall

REEDSBURG

Gerber Outlet
273 Main Street

Directions: Located in downtown Reedsburg on Highway 33
Phone: (608) 524–4347
Hours: 9:00 A.M.–5:30 P.M., Monday–Thursday; 9:00 A.M.–8:00 P.M., Friday; 9:00 A.M.–5:00 P.M., Saturday; 11:00 A.M.–3:00 P.M., Sunday
Credit Cards: No
Personal Checks: Yes, with driver's license
Handicapped Accessible: Yes
Food: Restaurants within walking distance
Bus Tours: Yes

RIPON

Fox River Glove Outlet Store
113 W. Fond Du Lac Street

Directions: Just off town square in downtown Ripon
Phone: No phone
Hours: 8:00 A.M.–8:00 P.M., Monday–Friday; 9:00 A.M.–5:00 P.M., Saturday; 10:00 A.M.–4:00 P.M., Sunday
Additional Savings: Summer sale first week in August, winter clearance during March
Credit Cards: MasterCard, Visa
Personal Checks: Yes, with proper identification
Handicapped Accessible: No
Food: Restaurants in downtown area several blocks away
Bus Tours: Yes

STEVENS POINT

Herrschner's Crafts, Inc.
2800 Hoover Road

Directions: Take Highway 51 to Highway 10 West exit; go west 1 block to Country Club Road. Turn left and go 1 mile to Hoover Road; turn left.
Phone: (715) 341–8686
Hours: 9:00 A.M.–5:00 P.M., Monday–Saturday; 11:00 A.M.–4:00 P.M., Sunday
Additional Savings: Annual warehouse sale Wednesday through Saturday of the third week of June
Credit Cards: American Express, MasterCard, Visa
Personal Checks: Yes, with proper identification
Handicapped Accessible: Yes
Food: One mile away
Bus Tours: Yes
Notes or Attractions: Factory tours with advance notice

WEST BEND

West Bend Outlet Mall
180 Island Avenue

Directions: Corner of Highway 33 and Island Avenue
Phone: (414) 334–3477
Hours: 9:30 A.M.–9:00 P.M., Monday–Friday; 9:30 A.M.–5:00 P.M., Saturday; 11:00 A.M.–5:00 P.M., Sunday
Additional Savings: Annual sale on Maxwell Street Day, first Wednesday of August
Outlets:
Ambrosia Chocolate & Cocoa
The Brighter Side
The Cookie Jar Cookie Outlet
Houseware Outlet Store
Kids by Rainbow Fashions
Little Red Shoe House
Maus Jewelry Imports
Newport Sportswear
Paper Factory
Rainbow Fashions
Regal Outlet Store
Trinkets 'n Treasures
West Bend Company Store
Winona Knits
Credit Cards: Most stores accept major credit cards.
Personal Checks: Yes, with proper identification
Handicapped Accessible: Yes, with one wheelchair available
Food: Food court in mall
Bus Tours: Yes
Notes or Attractions: Connected to downtown West Bend by a covered bridge over the Milwaukee River

PRODUCT INDEX

Clothing, Men's

Clothing, Men's Big and Tall

Clothing, Men's Careerwear/ Formal

Clothing, Men's Casualwear

Clothing, Outerwear

Clothing, Sweaters, Knit Goods

Clothing, Women's

OUTLET INDEX